Joetta's *P* Principles for Success

Joetta Clark Diggs
4 Time Olympian

Joetta's *P* Principles for Success

Life Lessons Learned from Track & Field

A Powerful Life Guide for You!

Joetta Clark Diggs
(1988, 1992, 1996 and 2000 Olympian)

Front & Back Cover Photograph: Mr. H. Hillard
Cover Design: Mrs. J. Yarka
Content Editor: Mrs. L. Fenner, Ms. L. Tucker, Mr. P. Kraus
Hair Stylist: Mrs. T. Alston

Send all book orders, appearances, and interview requests to
Joettaevents@yahoo.com

This book was printed in the United States of America.

To order additional copies of this book, contact:
Xlibris Corporation
1-888-795-4274
www.Xlibris.com
Orders@Xlibris.com
69940

Contents

Dedication

To my husband, Ronald, and daughter, Talitha
To my father, Joe, and mother, Jetta
To my brother, Joe "J. J.," and sister, Hazel "Peachy"
And to my relatives, friends, and everyone who encouraged or
inspired me to aim for the moon, always remembering that if,
by chance, I miss, I would land among the stars.

FOREWORD

Socrates was very specific about the interpersonal relationship between the mind and the physical being. In essence, he noted that a strong mind houses a strong body. Thus, the premise of this book by my daughter, Joetta Clark Diggs, is ensconced in the principles of her five Ps.

The primary focus of Joetta's philosophies is the fact that you must find your purpose, get prepared, be patient, get perturbed, and persevere as you find your raison d'être. Once you realize your reason for being, providence buoyed by a stubborn perseverance will catapult you into the methodical perfect cadence of success. However, if you do not find your reason for being, you will be miserable and unhappy.

Over the years, Joetta has found her raison d'être; and as a result, she has achieved incredible heights. The premise of her existence was predicated upon being the best she could become. Often, she referred to Ralph Waldo Emerson. He noted, "Oh what a tragedy to meet the point of death only to realize that you have not lived and not scratched the surface of your potential."

Joetta's P Principles for Success are the apotheosis of fulfilling your mission on this planet. Calvin Coolidge noted that "nothing can take the place of persistence, talent can not, geniuses can not and education can not."

Joetta's life as a college graduate, four-time Olympian, businesswoman, wife, and mother have been the quintessence of being the best of what you are capable of obtaining. Certainly, her achievements are noteworthy and deserving of emulation.

I believe that this book is a must-read for everyone. My daughter has created a sensible and powerful guide to overcoming obstacles as you pursue your success. Once you start the book, you will not want to put it down until you have developed strategies for the successful you. My only advice is that you read the book expeditiously.

Dr. Joe L. Clark

ACKNOWLEDGMENTS

I would like to acknowledge the many people who, for over ten years, asked me the question, "When are you going to write a book?" Your words have echoed in my mind for many years, and I thank you for being patient with me until I decided to finally put pen to paper.

To my mother, Jetta, and father, Joe—I thank you for knowing the importance of education, skills, character, and respect. My parents spent all of their lives developing their children into positive, kind, and respectful people. It is through them that I learned about sacrifice, being prepared, and being responsible for the choices that I made. My hope has been and will always be that I have made them proud, and they know that their guidance and love have always fueled me as I meandered my way through the maze of life.

To my husband, Ronald, whom I met on a blind date toward the end of my athletic career—his support, intelligence, and love for his family were a driving force behind this book being completed. When I did not know what to write, when to write, or how to write, I spoke with him or showed him my material, and he would simply utter these encouraging words, *"Just keep writing!"* That was all the motivation that I needed to continue with the book. So I thank you for caring enough not to void my spirit but rather encourage me to start the race to becoming an author and being there when I crossed the finish line.

To my daughter, Talitha, who is the reason I strive to better myself—because of her, I choose and will continue to live with integrity, hope, passion, character, and conviction. So when she thinks of these words, she will always think about me.

To my brother, J. J., who displayed endless support for me as his sister—for many years, he was always Joetta's little brother and never once flinched at that association growing up. He has been the calm during my storms and the wind beneath my wings. I thank him for understanding what it took to coach me as an elite athlete. His character, kindness, and tenacious work ethic have made him an outstanding; brother, husband, father, and coach who is well respected by many.

My sister, Hazel, who is 16 years my junior—I thank her for always cheering for me when she was little. Hazel did not know that she too would one day run the 800m. She also didn't know that I would, one day, cheer for her as she wrote her own name in the 800m history books. Hazel has always encouraged me to write a book especially when I shared various track-and-field stories with her. It was the look in her eyes, the questions that she asked, and the laughter that I heard from her that let me know which stories to use in my book. So thank you for being interested in my, those-were-the-good-old-day stories.

To my track & field age group coaches, Mr. Hooper, Mr. Long, Mr. Hickey, Mr. Potash, Mr. Wilson I thank you for allowing me to travel with you and keeping running fun for me. To Mr. Klepack, Mr. Cole, Mr. Moss, Mr. Gavitt, Mr. Brooks, Mr. Fred Thompson who were my high school coaches and they all prepared me for the next level. To my college coach Ms. Terry

Crawford who was my only female coach and showed me that a woman could be in charge, fair, tenacious, and successful. And to my competitors, agents, family, friends, fans, foes, mentors, and business partners, I thank each and every one of you for being in my life and providing me with experiences that made this book possible. And I thank God for never leaving or forsaking me as I traveled down my road of life. I will always believe and follow what the scripture says, "To whom much is given, much is required."

INTRODUCTION

Joetta's P Principles for Success is designed to help you reach your destiny. So often in life, we try to figure out what we are going to do, how we are going to do it, and why we are going to do it. We spend so much time trying to figure out the answers to these questions that we usually do not get anything done.

This book is meant to help you reach your destiny in life. I believe that where there is no vision, there is no victory, and where there is no victory, there is no celebration. I want you to be able to celebrate your life visions and your accomplishments. For years, I have lectured on the Ps: purpose, prepare, patience, perturbed, and persevere; and I have listened to people's comments regarding the effectiveness of these words and how, if utilized correctly, these words can change, direct, or reconfirm the path in which one travels to their success. The pages that you are about to read will outline the five Ps by using short track and business stories about my life. At the end of each chapter, I encourage you to carefully and thoughtfully participate in an exercise by answering questions.

As an athlete, I have learned how to set goals, stay focused, overcome obstacles, and discover the champion that exists within me. The lessons that I have learned in sports parallel the lessons learned in life. So as you read these stories, think about your life experiences and how you are going to use the five Ps to realize your success. You are just a few chapters away from your victory. So readers set! Now turn the page and I will meet you at the finish.

CHAPTER 1

Clear Vision

1st "P"

Purpose: An anticipated outcome that is intended or that guides your planned actions.

As long as I can remember, people have asked me about my purpose in life. I often wondered why people were so interested in my purpose and if having a purpose really mattered. On the other hand, since everyone wanted to know about purpose, what did it mean and how did I go about getting this purpose? Was it something that I would learn? Was it something that was given to me? Or was it something that could be developed? My experiences have led me to this belief about purpose. Purpose will vary for individuals and situations; but one thing is sure: without a purpose in life, you will be unable to reach your destiny. In other words, without a purpose in life, your contribution to others and yourself will go unnoticed.

At a very young age, I knew I enjoyed being around people, talking, competing, and challenging myself to be my very best. So I involved myself in sports, I performed as a ballet dancer, I spoke in front of people, I wrote, and I always helped people. It was my parents' belief that they were responsible for exposing their children to as many activities and experiences as possible. They wanted us to be complete individuals—well versed academically, athletically, and spiritually. Therefore, I worked hard in school and in sports, and I involved myself in church. I was constantly reminded that in order for me to compete in sports and take ballet and piano lessons, I had to maintain good grades. My parents always emphasized the importance of education and they had a clear vision as to how they were going to raise, nurture, and develop me into a responsible adult. I was going to follow the suggestions from adults—graduate from high school, graduate from college, compete in sports, have a talent, and be a kind, respectful human being. I learned about purpose, and my parents were an integral part of that equation.

How did I apply this knowledge to my life as an athlete? My parents always told me that in order to be successful, I must work hard, make sacrifices, and believe in myself. As a student at Columbia High School in Maplewood, New Jersey, I won all of my 880-yard to 800-meter races. In my senior year of 1980, I set a state record of 2:03.5 for 800m, which still remains twenty-nine years later in 2009. As a high school student, I often thought about making an Olympic team and winning a gold medal in a United States of America uniform. After all, many kids who compete in athletics dream of making an Olympic team in their respective sport. I can remember thinking how cool it would be to make the Olympic team as a high school athlete and march in the opening ceremony with athletes from all over the world. In 1980, even though I did not make the Olympic Team, I did finished seventh in the Olympic Trials finals, which was a fine showing for a high school athlete. I also was not devastated with my seventh-place finish because, for political reasons, the USA ended up boycotting the 1980 Olympic Games. Moreover, since I was young and had age on my side, I believed that I would be able to try out again for the Olympics in 1984. Mr. Len Klepack was my high school coach and he did not train me in a way that would have me exhausted in high school. In other words, he did not take the fun out of the sport or life out of my legs, which would allow me to run better in college. The media stated that I was one of the top recruits for both males and females in any sports because of my many scholarship offers. I eventually accepted a full scholarship to the University of Tennessee. My college years went by quickly, and upon graduation, I had become a fifteen-time All-American and nine-time National Collegiate College Association (NCAA) champion and gained a wealth of confidence in my ability. I also had the opportunity to witness for the first time a successful program being run by women. The Women's Athletic Director, Sports Information Director, coaches, trainers and interns where predominately women. This setting allowed me to observe women at work, in what was considered a male dominated field, as they become successful. During my years at the University of Tennessee the Women's Athletic programs were some of the best in the country. As a student/athlete I watched the staff, I took notes and I knew that I wanted to pattern myself after them.

In 1984, I defended my NCAA outdoor title and I again went to the Olympic Trials in 1984 in hopes of making the 1984 Olympic Team. I can remember thinking how awesome it would be to win a medal on American soil, preferably the gold medal, and singing the national anthem with tears rolling down my face. I had this vision already placed in my mind because I had seen other gold medalist display this type of emotion. I forgot to mention that I had also envisioned the crowd chanting those all-too-familiar letters U-S-A. However, 1984 would not be the year for me either, for I did not even make the semifinals. As I watched the finals of the 1984 USA Olympic Trials women 800m and saw women in the finals that I had beaten in the past, my body was consumed with disappointment, and I had to gather all of my strength just to watch the race. There is a song that states these words, "Kick them when they're up, kick them when they are down," and that is exactly what I did. I kicked myself when I was down by reflecting on my performance in 1980. I reminded myself that when, as a high school athlete, I made the finals of the Olympic Trials and placed seventh. I was also saddened because, after doing the math, I knew that I would be twenty-six years old, which, by the standards at that time, was old. Another reality became clear to me because I was not making enough money in the sport and would most likely have to retire or find a job while I continued to run four more years in the hope of making the 1988 Olympic Team.

My purpose was challenged day after day, and then finally, I decided that I would run one more year to redeem myself for not making the 1984 Olympic Team. I trained hard, remained focused, and made sacrifices as I tried to run fast to get a company to sponsor me, which would allow me to make money to support myself. However, all along, there was a voice that I heard speaking to me, telling me to start my business career. But in the back of my mind, I kept thinking, *What if?* I wanted one more try, one more sign that would provide me with a ray of hope to stay in the sport. And then it happened. I was on the European Circuit running the 800m, and I was having a good string of races. I went to Oslo, Norway, and competed in a big meet called the Bislett Games. I always wanted to run in this meet because for years I watched this meet on television and saw many Olympian greats such as Evelyn Ashford, Steve Ovett, Sebastian Coe, Mary Decker, Edwin Moses, Carl Lewis, and Jackie Joyner-Kersee compete in this meet. From that point on, it became my aspiration to run on that same track and to become part of such that rich athletic history.

Then the moment finally came in July 1985 when I began to warm up for the Bislett Games in Oslo, Norway. I was nervous, but it was good nervousness because I was still able to concentrate on the race. As I warmed up, my heart pounded more and more; and every time I saw an athlete whom I admired, I could feel my heart pounding faster. With every stride, I became more excited; and when I did my last stride, a calm feeling consumed my body, and I knew that I was ready. I can remember looking into the stands as I put on my spikes, thinking the ambiance and enthusiasm of the crowd were great. I heard the race starter say, "Runners set" in Norwegian. I then toed the line, and the next sound that I heard was the bang from the race starter's pistol. After finishing the two laps, I crossed the line in first place, and I ran personal record of 1:58.98. That was my first time running under two minutes in the 800. In my event, breaking two minutes was a huge accomplishment and made me not only a contender in the USA but in the world. When I saw the clock at the finish line, I could not believe the time. I looked at my two friends, Michael Franks, 400m runner, and Stanley Redwine, 800m runner; and they both smiled and nodded to confirm the time on the clock. I hugged them, I was given victory flowers from a meet volunteer, and I started my victory lap. It is customary to throw your victory flowers in the stands to a fan. However, throwing my flowers into the stands was not even an option as I jogged, waved, smiled, and stopped to sign autographs. I was consumed with the victory, the moment and finished my victory lap with my floral bouquet. Moreover, I had my answer to my retirement question. I should stay in the sport and not start my business career.

I can remember calling home to my father and brother, and they mentioned that they saw the women's 800m results from Oslo in the *USA Today* newspaper. They both said that they thought the results from my race, which stated that I had won and had run under two minutes, was a misprint. However, they hoped that the results were correct because they knew how hard I had trained and all of the effort I had put into reaching this landmark. If I had run that time in 2009, my family could have checked many places to confirm the results. However, one must remember that back in 1985, there were no computers to check the results immediately, no BlackBerrys; therefore, they had to believe the paper until I finally called home the next day. Since there is a six-hour time difference between USA and Norway, I did not call until 7:00 a.m. the next day, which was 1:00 p.m. in the United States. And by that time, they had already seen the results. After hanging up the phone from my family, I reflected on their comments, and I thought to myself that even though they joked about my time suggesting that it was a misprint, I did not lose hope and I focused on what I needed to accomplish to stay in the sport.

After the meet, I got a solid Nike contract, and this started my quest to becoming the best 800m runner I could be. I stayed in the sport and qualified for the 1988 Olympic Trials, and this time, I made the Olympic team. I took third place by the smallest of margins. I ran 1:59.93, and the fourth placer was Debbie Grant, who today is a true friend. Her time was 1:59.97. It was a dive to the finish line, and the scar my dive left is still visible on my left shoulder. I often say, had I not been presented with the small USA flag indicating that I made the 1988 Olympic Team at the end of the race, I would have remained sprawled over the track and the rest of the meet would have been held somewhere else. So at the age of 26, I finally made my first Olympic team, which brings me back to my purpose. I mentioned that I traveled, made the Olympic team, had a contract, graduated from college, and was about to buy my first house; but what was my purpose? I thought my purpose was to make the Olympic team and get a medal. When that did not happen, my purpose changed to getting a big contract. The change occurred because, like many people, my purpose was not really a purpose but rather a goal. My goal was to make the Olympic team, graduate, win meets, and travel;

and my *purpose*, when it was all said and done, was to maximize my talent, thus allowing me to achieve the goals that I set for myself in sports, business, and family.

Questions:

1. Have you set a purpose for yourself?

2. Prior to reading this chapter, what was your purpose (in one specific area)?

3. What are you going to do to achieve this purpose? Phrase your goal as an objective.

4. After reading this chapter, what is your purpose?

5. What are you willing to do to achieve your purpose?

6. How do you feel about yourself when you feel you are not fulfilling your purpose? Why?

7. Name five positive characteristics about yourself. Name five characteristics that others might use to describe you. Identify any that are common. Do you agree with their assessment? Why or why not.

8. Name a situation where you did not follow through with an intended purpose. What held you back from pursuing your purpose? Fear? Insecurity?

9. As you progress through life, did you ever attempt the situation again?

CHAPTER 2

Get Ready Anyway

2ND "P"

Prepare: Getting ready beforehand for some purpose, use, or activity.

For over 28 years, I have traveled the world, and I have had the opportunity to meet wonderful people. As a young girl, I never thought that by competing in sports, I would eventually receive a full college scholarship, graduate from the University of Tennessee, visit many beautiful countries, and meet wonderful people from all over the world. However, if you live long enough, you will surely come to realize that you might not know where your travels will take you, but it is imperative that you prepare as best you can. In other words, by preparing and retaining information, you will allow yourself to soar like an eagle through various experiences and accomplish your goals.

When I was in middle school, I took French as my foreign language. The main reason that I selected French was simple; my parents took Spanish, and I did not want to have one more subject in which they could assist or understand. So French would be my subject, which meant no help from my parents. As a student trying to master this language, I studied hard, I listened to French lessons on albums that I played on a record player, and I also did my homework. All of this work was done hoping that one day I would speak French fluently. I was 13 years old; and basically, the only things I knew about France were Paris was the capital, France was where fashion *reigned*, and the Arc de Triomphe was important in France's history. I never imaged that in 1979, at the age of 16, I would make my first USA senior team and travel overseas on a nonstop flight to where else? Paris, France!

I was very excited about my trip abroad because I had taken French for three years, and I was confidently thinking that I had a good grasp on that language. So with my passport, translation book, cassette Walkman, DVDs, iPods, and MP3 players had not yet been invented in 1979, camera, clothes, snacks, hair supplies, family pictures, and of course my spikes, I left for my venture. The American team had the entire back half of the plane, which was great because we moved freely without worrying about people complaining. Most of my teammates were either in college or competing as open athletes on the track-and-field circuit and had been overseas before. However, they had never been on a flight that allowed them this much freedom. I too was so excited about the seating arrangement and freedom that I did not have time to get nervous. Moreover, the older athletes had already decided to take me under their wings, and I had been prepped by my parents, so I felt safe. As a novice athlete, my plans were set for the trip: simply observe, enjoy, compete well and appreciate the experience. During the six-hour flight, I had a difficult time sleeping because I was overwhelmed with excitement. I could not wait to see the sights, meet the people, prepare for the competition, and of course, send postcards home.

After arriving at the airport, clearing customs, and riding the bus to the hotel, one thing became apparent—the French that I learned in school was so foreign that even the French people could not understand a word I was saying. In addition, they spoke so quickly, I could not understand them either. I found myself often using all sorts of hand language and exaggerated facial expressions in hopes of communicating better with the locals. During this agonizing time, every now and then, someone would put me out of my misery and would say in a strong but friendly accent, "I speak English." As I reflect on that moment in my life, one word comes to my mind—*prepared*. I truly was not prepared to speak with the French people, and my only hope was that this lack of preparation would not transfer to my running.

The next day, in spite of the communication barrier between myself and the French, I still decided to venture out alone to see the sites around the perimeter of the hotel. It was then that I had a revelation. I discovered that all was not lost; and since I was able to read and understand the written language, thus, I could interpret the signs, menus, and read the newspaper. So there *was* a reason that I studied French after all. I could be an interpreter for myself and others. As I continued walking, a smile came across my face because I realized that I had made the best of a situation going bad. My mother always said, "If you are given lemons, learn how to make lemonade." At that moment, I truly understood what she meant by that statement.

Our hotel was in Bourges, France, a small city outside of Paris. We had our practices at a local track, and I can vividly remember the people coming out to watch the Americans work out. Many of the track stadiums in Europe can seat more than 25,000 people, and the stadiums remind me of the USA football stadiums. This stadium was a little smaller, but the crowd would be close to the track, and we would be able to really hear the cheering.

The track & field competition against the French was scheduled for a couple of days after our arrival. In the meantime, our team manager scheduled a bus tour around Paris. The bus tour took us to several locations; I saw two of the three Statue of Liberty replicas that are in France. Two of the statues are in Paris: one is located in the Seine River, and the other one is located in Jardin du Lexembourg, a large park. The third Statue of Liberty replica is located in Bordeaux, a city in Southwest France. In my history class, I learned that the French gave America the original Statue of Liberty. I can honestly state that I had not done enough research, which is another way of saying that I was not prepared, and I was completely surprised to see two of the three smaller Statue of Liberty replicas in France. I was, however, familiar with some of the other sites such as the Eiffel Tower, the Arc de Triomphe, the Louvre Museum, and the Notre Dame Cathedral. I enjoyed the bus trip and took many pictures during our guided tour.

There came a time during our trip that the staff gave us some time to go out on our own. Our USA coaches suggested that we go out in small groups. My group was comprised of four people including myself, and we had a great time. We shopped, took pictures, enjoyed the scenery, and tasted many different pastries. We were having a wonderful time until we noticed that we were lost. The group did not panic too much because we thought that we had plenty of time to get back to the bus. However, once we realized that we only had about 25 minutes to return to the bus, we lost our composure. In the midst of this panic, I tried my best to use my broken French to communicate. I quickly became frustrated because no matter how hard I tried to engage in some type of conversation, I could not understand much of what was being said. Then suddenly, we saw someone whom we thought could help us. We ran across the street, shouting in English, "Excuse me! Excuse me!" Once we got the man's attention, we all began asking him for directions at once. However, he just stood there looking at us and not answering our questions. Finally, someone showed him the paper and pointed to the written address. We were proud of ourselves because we were somewhat prepared. At least, we had the location of the parked tour bus. But nothing could have prepared us for what happened next. The man turned around and started speaking to us in French. Our mouths dropped wide-open. No one made this comment at that time, but at that moment, I am sure we were all thinking, *How could this be? You must be kidding me.* We simply could not believe that this man, who was not just any man because he resembled my father, could not speak English. At that time, I did not think how arrogant and naive we were to expect all black people to speak English even if we are in another country.

As we walked away from the man, we giggled because we were embarrassed and nervous as we wondered how we were going to get back to the bus. We also discussed the fact that we had hoped this man spoke English because we were lost. We commented on his skin color, which helped give us a false sense of hope to our problem. We also noted that for the remainder of our trip, we would be more mindful of other people's cultures. We continued walking as we argued and blamed each other for being in this current predicament. During this time, I also made it known that I was in high school, which gave me an automatic excuse, thus excluding me from any blame. I simply kept saying, "I am holding all of you accountable for this embarrassing moment because, after all, you are *college students*." I felt really good using this defense because my younger siblings used that excuse against me on many occasions. And in a strange way even though I knew better, I liked the power associated with blaming the older people; and for that moment, I wished that I were the youngest person all of the time.

We continued walking around, not knowing where to go. In retrospect, I wish BlackBerrys, cell phones, and text messaging and GPS devices had been invented in 1979 because these items would have helped us to get to our destination. However, it would be many years before that technology became available. Finally, we heard someone call out in English, "Are you guys lost?" We looked across the street and saw some of our American teammates. We were ecstatic to see them, and we ran across the street, greeting them with laughs and hugs. This group took us directly to the bus. As we followed them back to the bus, my group told them of our experience, and our story quickly became the talk of the trip. We arrived to the hotel safely, and the rest of the evening, I could not help but think that in the midst of all the excitement and the fun, I hoped that everyone would be prepared to compete in a couple of days.

On race day, the competition turned out to be very exciting as I watched both teams put everything they had into their performances. Even though I was there to compete, I think that I was just as intrigued as the spectators with the enthusiasm they displayed for the athletes. At the age of 16, I had not seen that many people at a track meet outside of Penn Relays in Philadelphia, Pennsylvania, and the Olympics on television. When the final races were finally complete, the Americans had a fine showing, setting records and winning races. I was excited because my 4x800-meter relay set an American record of 8:19.9. The first leg was run by Olympian Robin Campbell a San Jose State College graduate, ran 2:04.5. I ran the second leg at 2:04.1; Chris Gregorek, a Georgetown University graduate, ran third with 2:06.5; and Essie Kelley, a Prairie View University graduate anchored in 2:04.8. Our time was set on June 24, 1979, and remained an American record for twenty-eight years and was broken at Penn Relays in 2008.

As I flew back to the United States, I reflected on my experiences. There were many things that I was not prepared for. I was not prepared for the culture, the language barrier, or the overall

French history. I missed my family because I was not able to call home on a regular basis. At that time, texting and Skype were not an option. When I wanted to call home, I had to call the AT&T operator and make a collect call. However, my parents had already informed me that I could only call upon arrival, after my race, when I was in the airport to come home. My parents always said, "No news was good news." So that was the premise that I operated under even in Europe.

What was my purpose? The primary reason for me going over to Paris as a sixteen-year-old was to represent the USA. I think I accomplished that goal—my team won the competition, we set an American record, and I ran the fastest split on the relay. But in the process, I learned about French culture, which helped me understand the importance of becoming aware of your surrounds. After reassessing the trip, I concluded that I was prepared for something after all. I gained a greater respect for life outside of the United States of America, and I knew that I wanted to visit Europe again.

As an athlete, I have so many interesting track experiences and countless track stories, many of which will be shared with you throughout these chapters. However, I think it is also important for me to share the business component of the *P* principles.

At the beginning of the book, I mentioned that track and life had many parallels and the character and lessons learned in sports can be relevant in business. In 1988, I was contacted by a school to speak and that is how I began my career as a speaker. I did not know that some 20 years later, I would be considered as a renowned motivational speaker who would deliver team enrichment and health & wellness presentations to companies, universities, and other organizations across the world. In an earlier sentence, I used the word *embark*, which would lead one to think that I planned and set out to have groups bring me in as their speaker. However, it was just the antithesis.

I can honestly say that my speaking career began when I returned from making the 1988 Olympic Team in Seoul, South Korea. A school wanted me to speak to their students about my first Olympic experience. However, they did not have any money in the school's budget for this program. I always viewed myself as a role model, and I said yes to the question. I was thrilled that someone thought that I had something worthwhile to say. I conducted two assemblies at the school. I can remember speaking, making jokes, answering a vast array of questions from the children and signing autographs. During the program, I also asked students questions, and they knew the answers, which impressed me very much because I can remember being a student and taking naps during an assembly program. So with that in mind, I tried to keep the presentation interesting hoping not to find any students sleeping.

When I left the school, I thought that I could conduct more of these sessions if I were to *prepare* myself. I enjoyed the experience, and the applauses confirmed, at least in my mind, that the students also enjoyed my presentation. So I began thinking about my life and jokes and remembering track stories. Then I combined track stories from my third grade-college academic experiences and started developing topics for my presentations. This process was the beginning of preparing for my speaking engagement success in the future. I then began receiving phone calls from groups asking me to speak. I said yes to all the calls because I knew that I needed to gain experience in this area if I wanted to make speaking a full-time career. Therefore, I committed to delivering speeches to audiences at no charge to gain the experience I needed to be able to, one day, command an honorarium. So often in life, we want money, and that is the driving force behind what we are doing.

However, I have always maintained that if you are *prepared*, have a product that others desire and if you are proficient in that area, opportunities and income will follow.

I saw that I was being sought after by groups, and I developed a name and decided to start my own business, thus the beginning of Joetta Sports & Beyond, LLC. Again, we sometimes miss opportunities because we are not prepared, and then we want to blame someone else for our shortcomings. As it relates to my life, I never want to get denied due to the lack of preparation on my part. My parents always said that it is better to be prepared for an opportunity and not have the opportunity than be unprepared. Terry Crawford who was my college coach had another saying that was similar to my parents saying. She said, "You never have a second time to make a first impression." So from that day on in November 1988 to the present, I have developed and delivered countless presentations, and the only difference from my first program at the middle school to now is that I can command an honorarium and I feel confident about my work and the message being presented to the audience.

We have to believe that we were all put on earth for a purpose and when you step out on faith. You must believe in yourself, and you cannot be afraid to take risks. My first school assembly presentation to children was successful despite not having a speaker's resume, PowerPoint presentation, a videos, pictures, props, or agents. I simply knew that I enjoyed speaking to people and I believed that just because you might fail or not accomplish your immediate goal doesn't mean that you are a failure.

Preparation is important, and we must be fearless as we prepare for the success and riches that await us. Always remember that you might not understand why you are experiencing or learning something, but you must hold on to your vision. In other words, "Prepare and get ready anyway."

Through the stories in this chapter, I have talked about being prepared and the importance of getting ready for opportunities long before they happened. The following questions will help you understand your purpose and challenge you to get prepared for your success.

1. Identify a situation that initially seemed like a daunting task but later proved to be beneficial to you.

2. Discuss how you are going to *prepare* for one of your goals.

3. Name an aspect of your life that you're *prepared* for and describe how this preparation helped you to be successful in another situation. List the steps required to reach your goal.

4. Using the purpose you wrote down from the proceeding chapter; explain how you are going to prepare for that purpose.

CHAPTER 3

"Not Yet! Says Who?"

3RD "P"

Patience: The state (amount) of enduring in a decision-making process without becoming upset or annoyed.

As a little girl growing up, I can remember wanting to be a model, a news personality, or anyone that would be featured in the media. I think, as youngsters, we all wanted to have our names appear in lights. We all had visions of how our fame would play out, and we were not concerned with people's negative comments regarding our dreams. At a young age, I certainly knew what I wanted. I wanted a bigger house, I wanted to wear fancier clothes, I wanted my picture on the cover of magazines/ billboards, I wanted to travel, and I wanted to be on television. I really desired all of this since I was very young and really did not comprehend all of the issues surrounding that time. I was able to hold fast to my dreams. Those years proved to be very difficult for people because of much civil unrest and gender inequities that constantly had women struggling to prove their value at home, in the workplace, and in society. There were also the 1967 riots that devastated many cities across the country. It was a decade of upheaval and change involving not only black activism but also growing antiwar sentiment, street theater aimed at social change and class conflict, and the beginning of a women's rights movement. But in the midst of all that was going on around me, I had questions, I received answers, and I remained hopeful and patient, never doubting that better days lie ahead.

I mentioned that as a youngster, I was very curious, and I often asked my parents questions such as why some people treated others unjustly and why individuals boycotted and marched. I can vividly remember Dr. Martin Luther King's "I have a dream" speech and some of the points in the speech. My parents reviewed many of his visions with us, and we often had interesting family discussions. Regardless of what we talked about, my parents constantly reminded me of this one point: "No matter what, never let anyone discourage you from your dreams. And remember that just because someone has never done something before, it doesn't mean that you cannot accomplish it." These words left an indelible mark in my mind, and some forty years later, I still hear their conversations echoing when I attempted new ventures.

With my parents' words and my goals ingrained in my brain, I set out to make contributions to society regardless of the events and mind-sets of the people during 1960s, '70s, '80s, or '90s. I would not be distracted or defeated; I would simply use the situations to fuel my steps as I waited patiently for great results. My parents instilled in me to never think about how something would happen, but instead to simply get ready and be poised while navigating through what I now call the "Not yet! Says who?" maze.

Over the years, I have learned that our childhood forces us to deal with and find solutions to the problems we encounter as youngsters. I know that many children of my generation had no other option than to figure out the solutions to problems on their own. Our parents would not shelter us or come to our rescue for every single problem. Our parents allowed us to work through situations with our peers, and most of the time, we were friends again with the child we had the disagreement with before the streetlights came on. The streetlights coming on indicated that it was time to come inside for dinner, and everyone knew not to ignore the streetlights. I can remember coming home and telling my parents that kids poked fun at me because I was thin, my hair was short, and my skin was permanently tan. My parents would simply say, "You better love yourself because God made you, and God doesn't make any junk!" So as I was confronted and teased, I remembered that phrase; and in times of confrontation, I repeated that phrase to myself to gather strength required to work through that moment. I would like to say that I did not tease anyone, but the truth of the matter is that I also, on occasions, dished out mean comments.

While I was in high school, my athletic career began to develop resulting in my name and picture constantly appearing in the *Star-Ledger* newspaper, which is the largest circulated newspaper in the state of New Jersey. People often joked around and said that my family must pay the reporters because I was always featured in articles. My success on the track even influenced the paper to create a headline specifically for me. Instead of the headline reading, "Columbia's Clark," it often read, "Clark's Columbia." I began to see parts of my dream develop. People were now reading about me and seeing my name and picture in the paper.

As I read the articles and saw my name in the paper every week, I felt good despite comments some schoolchildren made to me. I was described as having spider legs, shiny skin, and Afro hair. However, none of those remarks seemed to matter anymore; and I even discovered that the more media attention I received, the more friends I acquired. By my sophomore year in high school, the negative comments stopped altogether. I now found myself wanting to be on the cover of magazines and announce sporting events. But during my childhood and high school years, there were not many people on magazine covers or, for that matter, in magazine periods that looked like me. So for years, I kept my dreams to myself ever; and even though society said "Not yet!" in my mind, I faintly heard the words "Says who?"

Somehow, twenty years of my life had passed; I was over thirty, I had no billboard, and my picture had not been on a cover of a magazine. However, I did realize some of my childhood dreams. I had graduated from college, purchased a house, traveled around the world, had fancier clothes, and started my business. I would simply have to remain patient for my billboards and magazine covers to become a reality. I just had to remember that I could not move forward if I was looking backward. Instead, I had to remember to hold on to my dreams and continue pressing forward toward my goals in life.

Throughout my life, many of my friends constantly teased me because I seemed to somehow learn about things before many of them. I often shared this information with my friend Connie Price-Smith, who made four Olympic teams with me. The first question out of her mouth was "How did you know that?" followed by "I know, Joetta, you were just minding your business, and it fell upon your ears," I would chuckle and say, "That is right. I was minding my own business."

Then one day, when I was minding my own business, that was the saying I would use to preface any information I was about to reveal, and somehow, I found out that Nike was looking for an Olympian to promote their 1996 clothing line for the 1996 Olympic Games, being held in Atlanta, Georgia. I remembered calling my agent with such enthusiasm because I thought I was the perfect person for this Nike advertisement. At that point in my career, I had been a Nike-sponsored athlete for about eleven years. I was in great physical shape, I had the athletic body, and I was over 30 years old, which was the very market that Nike was targeting with this new campaign.

During the conversation, I informed my agent that Nike needed a model for this campaign, and I wanted him to contact Nike on my behalf. The next words that I heard from his mouth had such an impact; it felt like I had just been hit by a freight train. His exact words were, "You did not go to an Ivy League school." I remembered taking the receiver away from my mouth and looking at it as though it were the face of my agent. I thought to myself, *I wish I could reach my hand through the phone and pop him for making that ridiculous statement.* After hearing his words, I became defensive and said, "What does graduating from an Ivy League school have to do with being a model." It was not as if I was asking him to get me into Oxford on a Rhodes Scholarship. I refused to remain on the phone, and have any pride that I had left sucked right out of me. He could detect that I was upset; however, when he heard the dial tone, that confirmed his suspicion. When I dejectedly hung up the phone, one thing was crystal clear. He could no longer represent me because his comment indicated that he did not believe in me, and I was convinced that he would not fight hard for me when negotiating my contracts. In life, people must be sure to surround themselves with individuals who have their best interest at heart, and all others have to be held at bay.

Afterward, I made some pity party calls to share my story. After speaking with people, I managed to gather enough courage to call Nike myself. Why did I do that? The person said that Nike was looking for a high-profile athlete. My pride was crushed again. How could he say that to me? After all, I had waited patiently for this moment, and I thought I *was* a high-profile athlete. I had American and World records—I had made the 1988 and 1992 Olympic Team, I was ranked the best American in the 800m in 1992, and I was in a perfect position to make my third at the 1996 Olympic Trials. As I hung up the phone after hearing yet another rejection, it was then that I remembered the words from my childhood: "Not yet! Says who?" The very thought of those words once again gave me the strength to immediately call my agent and inform him that I would no longer need his services. Afterward, I reminded myself to be patient, for good things come to those who wait. Over the next months, I trained harder and was going to make everyone involved in the situation know that a mistake had been made and that I *was* a high-profile American athlete.

About two weeks later, I received a call from Nike; and they said, "Joetta, we would like to use you for the campaign, you will have a life-size poster of yourself in all Lady Foot Locker stores, and you will have sneakers, magazines, and yes, billboards." Well, I was so excited I could not wait to do the photo shoot. When the photos and ads finally hit the newsstand, I got many calls. The ad featured me in a side running shot in a running position in Nike's new workout gear. It was a black high-rise shorts and black front-zipped midriff top with short sleeves. It was quite fashionable for the mid-1990s. My motto was also attached to the ad, which read, "She speaks softly, but carries a big kick." During my career, I was known among other running strategists for my strong sprint over the last 100m.

I got calls from friends saying congratulations. I got a call from Nike stating that the campaign was a huge success. After the campaign was finished, my mother went to every Lady Foot Locker store she could find, trying to collect the life-size poster of her daughter.

In June of 1996, I made the USA Olympic Team in the women's 800m with a time of 1:58.22. What a great feeling to have made my third Olympic team and to have had the opportunity to compete in the Olympics in my country in front of a home crowd. The Olympics were to be held in Atlanta, Georgia, and the city was preparing to be on center stage for about two weeks. All of the Olympic signage security, hotels, restaurants, and novelty stores were working hard in anticipation of huge crowds. I was also excited because I was about to realize my childhood dream of becoming a model. The Nike ad that I shot back in May 1996 was about to be launched in magazines, billboards, and posters for all to see. And today, when I am in my house and see the life-size 1996 Nike ad featuring me and the saying "I run with a big kick," I sometimes reflect on everything that happened to make my dream a reality, and I smile as I think about my saying, "Not yet! Says who?" I smile because I am proud to know that despite the trials and tribulations I faced, I still managed to become triumphant.

In 2000, I made my fourth Olympic team and retired after the Olympic Games in Sydney, Australia. Even though my athletic career was over, I will always be proud of my ability to navigate through my maze of life by having a purpose, getting prepared, and being patient. After all, patience is needed if you are going to ever reach your goals and discover the champion that is in you. Sometimes, you want everything all at once, and with that mind-set, you are not able to plant the seeds of success, which only grow with the tribulations of life. I was 38 years old when I made my fourth Olympic team. Since my career had a span of over twenty-five years, I was the older woman in the 800m. However, whenever I was asked when I was going to retire, my answer consistently was, "Do not ask me when I am going to retire. Ask the younger women who I just beat when are they going to retire."

During the patience stage, you have to be willing to meander your way through the trials and tribulations of situations in order to become triumphant. It is during this moment of valor that you can say, "Not yet, says who?" because that which was deemed impossible by others was accomplished by you.

1. Name a dream you had as a child that you saw come to fruition as an adult.

2. What phrase or words do you use to help you remain patient during trials and tribulations?

3. Think of an area in your life and use the three Ps: purpose, preparation, and patience that you have learned so far to help you through this exercise.

4. Create a motto that describes your philosophy/approach to life. Explain why.

5. Discuss a situation that required you to be patient, but you instead chose to rush through the matter.

6. Did you have positive or negative results? Explain your answer.

CHAPTER 4

Don't Worry Who Pushed You In

Just Get Out

Perturbed: Becoming agitated, alarmed, or upset due to a situation.

If you live long enough, you will surely find yourself in a situation that will test your resolve and your commitment to success. When I am in a predicament, I usually try to find a rational solution to the problem. However, I have come to the conclusion that being rational might not be the best solution for a particular situation. You might also find out that there are times when all the education, self-talk, faith, mommilies, and affirmations can seem to fail you in your search to be rational. When pressures bear down on you, these times become the defining moments of a true champion. It is during these times that a champion somehow taps into their inner self and finds a way to overcome the insurmountable hurdles that appears to have one goal—to push you down to the ground, never once letting up until you lie lifeless on the ground of the defeated.

A champion gets angry and upset, but they eventually conquer all fears and doubts because champions understand that when they become perturbed, no option is left but to succeed. So the question remains. Have you ever been perturbed? What did you do in the midst of the situation that left you just enough air to continue to become victorious?

In 1985, I had just run my best time in the 800m of 1:58.98 in a race over in Europe. I was excited and thought that I was about to realize one of my track-and-field dreams. However, when I went to my agent and asked him if I could stay in Europe to compete on the second-half circuit, he smiled, shook his head, and said, *no*. Although I heard his response, the word did not really resonate with me because my eyes were fixated on his smile. However, in the midst of me looking at his smile, I thought that I heard the words, "No, you cannot stay because I cannot get you into any races in the second half." I asked him why he could not get me into races and proceeded to tell him the obvious about my performances and my times. To add insult to injury, I heard some Santa Monica athletes mention that they were going to compete in other races, and I mentioned that to him. But my agent did not seem concerned, sympathetic, or interested in my case at all. He simply said that Santa Monica is a powerful male-dominated team with athletes such as Carl Lewis, Johnny Gray, Leroy Burrell, Mike Marsh, Kirk Baptiste among others, and the meet directors will take all of Santa Monica's athletes regardless of their rankings to secure the team superstars' participation in their meets.

After hearing his unacceptable explanation for why he could not get me into the meets and why I would need to return to the States, I became perturbed and walked away from the situation. During my walk back to the bus, my joy from winning the race slowly turned into defeat. I felt as if no one was representing me effectively and presenting a case for me to stay in Europe to run the next race. As I thought and analyzed my predicament, I found it hard to believe that even though I had just run the race of my life, set a personal record, beat most of the best women 800m runners in the world at that time, in his mind, that was not good enough for him to present my case to a meet director. After the competition, all of the athletes were shuttled back to the meet hotel by bus. During the bus trip, people were congratulating me; but their comments fell upon deaf ears as I stared out the window, feeling dejected.

When I got to my room, a waterfall of tears was unleashed from my eyes. I spoke to myself saying, "Stop it! Crying will not make it better." There are times in your life that you will have to talk to yourself to get your feet on solid ground and to deal with the situation. Suddenly, I felt the strength in my body come back again as I thought through the problem. Yes, it was OK for me to be upset, but I still had options to explore. I could turn the anger and disappointment into something positive, or I could remain frustrated and pack up my bags and go home. In my moment of being perturbed, it became very clear to me that my agent did not care whether I stayed in Europe or went home because he had already answered my question without having a conversation with the meet director. I thought, *You have some nerve telling me to go home.* His lack of interest helped me to focus on the situation. So often in life we lose perspective of our vision, and we simply complain to others and spend much negative energy accomplishing nothing. But I was not going to conduct myself that way. At that instance, I knew exactly what had to be done.

I can remember running to my friend Candy's room. Candy made the 1980 Olympic Team for the 100m hurdles. I began telling her my situation and, more importantly, my plan. After discussing everything with Candy, I asked if she was going to come with me. I did not wait for an answer. I left her room; and by the time I reached the elevator, Candy was standing beside me, giggling and shaking her head in disbelief. Candy later mentioned that she did not know what I was going to do, but she needed to be there to save me from myself. Candy mentioned that she thought I was crazy because athletes, especially neophytes, were not supposed to impose themselves on big European meet directors. As we walked down the corridor that appeared to get longer and longer toward the meet director's room, Candy almost talked me out of my plans. At that time, I remembered what my parents said, "Just because something has never been done before doesn't mean that you cannot do it." While we walked down the hallway, Candy asked if I knew which room belonged to the meet director. I said, "yes." She then said, "How do you know?" I mentioned that I saw the agents lining up outside of the door earlier that day. In those days, the agents would form a line outside of the door of the meet directors to discuss the negotiations of their athletes. After answering the last question from Candy, I suddenly gave my friend a frowning expression and shook my head, which was an indication that I wanted her to stop asking questions. We finally finished our walk down the hall and eventually stood in front of the door. I knocked on the door firmly and quickly before I had time to rethink my intensions. A tall man with a cigar in his mouth answered the door with a blank stare on his face that assured me that he had no idea who we were. I said in a strong voice while extending my hand for him to shake, "My name is Joetta Clark from the US, and I won the race today with a personal best of 1:58.98, and I really do not want to go home." I had decided that I only had one chance, and I was going to make my entire presentation before he had an opportunity to speak. I continued by stating, "I would rather run in your meet than any other meets during the second half." There was a short pause; he looked at Candy and me and then said with a deep voice in a heavy accent, "OK, there is a chartered plane leaving tomorrow. Be on the 7:30 a.m. bus to the airport." I shook my head and said thank you as I backed out of the entranceway. We left the room and bolted down the hallway to the elevator before it finally hit me what I had done. When we got to Candy's room, we laughed about what just transpired and how we could not believe how easy that was and that I had been only moments from being on my way home.

The next morning, I was one of the first athletes on the chartered bus to the airport, and I was excited to have a seat on the short flight. I checked in my room, and of course, Candy was my roommate. After we got settled into our room, we went to eat lunch. This is the first time I saw my agent since he gave me my flight information to go home. He look surprised to see me, but it was me this time that had the broad smile as I spoke. I told him that I no longer needed his services and informed him that I was in all of the second-half meets. He did not believe me, and he asked how I was able to accomplish that feat. I smiled, and Candy and I both giggled as he walked away. The smile that he saw on my face was the only expression that I could display at the time because I hoped that it would remind him of the smile he gave to me upon telling me that I had to go home. However, there is a bigger lesson here than the smile. One must realize that every smile is not a prediction of the now, but rather a forecast of the future. This smile had nothing to do with him; the smile was an investment into my future. The reality is that my future in Europe was uncertain, and it depended on my next race. Since I had not asked any of the other meet directors if I could compete in their meet, the only thing I knew was that I had to run a good race on competition day to move on to the next meet, and I was up for the challenge. It is important to smile in times of uncertainty because the smile becomes the hope and strength that you will need to achieve your goal.

I had a good race, and I made sure I saw the meet director. As I approached him, my broad smile let him know that I ran well. I did not have to say a word, and he assured me that my performance at his meet had assured me a lane in the remaining meets. In hindsight, he probably thought I wanted an appearance fee to compete in his meet. But little did he know that I was not even thinking about money. I only wanted a lane so I could run again and better my time. I was very excited and proud that I was proactive in this case and had the talent to put a good run together. Again, I ran under two minutes for the 800m. My time for that race was 1:59. I was on a roll that year, for I constantly ran under two minutes. To this day, I am the only American to run the 800m under two minutes every year for fifteen consecutive years.

Candy and I have continued our great friendship and we still laugh at that defining moment in my life because it took courage, confidence, and a commitment to a vision to not be afraid to step out and do something that had never been done before. My father always said that a person in earnest cannot be concerned with consequences.

I believe that it is OK to get perturbed, but when you are in that mind-set, do not complain, blame others, or lose hope in your ability. Instead, find something that will empower you to step out with certainty and be willing to find the answer to your situation.

I once heard about a wealthy man who loved alligators so much that he put them in his pool. Whenever he had company over to visit, he would challenge someone to jump in the pool; and if they made it across safely, they could have whatever possession of his they wanted. This one day, he had eight guests over and presented his challenge to the group. No one answered him, so they all started to walk away. As the group took about ten steps, they heard a splash; and when they turned around, they saw someone swimming frantically in the water as if their life depended on it. The group looked and began to cheer in amazement as the man swam to escape the jaws of the alligators. As the man got out of the water, the group began to applaud him. The homeowner said, "What do you want?" The man, who was breathing very hard and gasping for air, finally said, "I want—" And then he paused to take another breath before finishing his question. He then continued, "What I want to know is, who pushed me into the water?"

Like the guest at the gentleman's home, we will all get pushed into the water and will have no other option but to make it out safely. Even though we will get perturbed, we must be determined not to worry about "who pushed us in the water." We have to be more concerned with getting out.

1. Name a situation that you were perturbed for being "pushed into the water."

2. How did you get out?

3. Name another situation when you were perturbed for being pushed into something and you did not get out.

4. Discuss why you did not get out.

5. What were the ramifications of you not getting out?

CHAPTER 5

"You Have No Option Just Keep Going"

Persevere: Going through a hard time without giving up.

I am sure that you all have heard of the story about the tortoise and the hare. It would appear that a hare would win any race against a tortoise because the hare is the faster animal, but as we all know from the fable, the hare got off to a fast start and, feeling overly confident, decided to take a nap. While the hare napped, the ever-so-steady tortoise kept an even pace. The hare woke up just in time to see the tortoise cross the line first. I can just imagine how the hare must have felt losing to a slow-moving tortoise in the lead. I am sure the hare thought she was the superior talent because she possessed all of the modern technology that got her in condition to win the competition. But sometimes, the very people with all of the equipment, coaches, and therapists to make them successful lack a key component which is focus. This characteristic enables you to accomplish your goals. I often say that, "hard work beats talent when talent does not work hard." So in the game of life, what really matters is your ability to maximize your skills and talents. Always remember that becoming successful is not a sprint, but rather a marathon. You have to be willing to work hard and stay the course despite that discouraging voice or situation that might blindside you. You have to be determined enough to take control of your situation and continue to tell yourself, *Failure is not an option. It is just a nagging reality that keeps you focused.* You must also realize that sometimes in life, *You have no option just keep going.*

My track & field career started when I was about nine years old in the city of Newark. I would run the 50 and 100-yard dashes (we were not running meters in the early '70s) at my camp's field days. I competed for the Essex County Park Commission's (ECPC) camp at Weequahic Park in New Jersey. My camp would compete against other county parks in several sports—track & field, softball, kickball, archery, volleyball, basketball, tennis, and ping-pong, just to name a few events. I would win the sprints, and my team would win whatever sport we competed in because we had talented athletes, we worked as a team, and we had confidence. Be it softball where I was the pitcher on the coed team or volleyball where I would spike the ball by using my jumping ability, we would always beat our competitors. I enjoyed competition, winning, and of course, singing the victory chants that we prepared because we knew that we would win. When we sang our victory chants, our defeated opponents who stayed on their side would glare at us as if they were going to attack us at any moment. The longer they looked, the louder and more obnoxious we became until finally our camp counselors told us to quiet down and to begin the customary handshaking. The handshake could not have been fun for the opposing team especially after having heard and watched our team's victory celebration.

It was during these fun times at the field day competition that I became interested in competing in the Olympics. I wanted to be a famous sprinter like Wilma Rudolph, 1960 gold medalist at 100m, 200m and the 4x100m relay. I wanted to run on the Americans' 4x100m relay. I had visions of me receiving the baton from my teammate and anchoring my team down the homestretch to a USA team victory. After which, we would jog our victory lap, waving the USA flag. I would have been prepared because I had plenty of experience from taking victory laps and participating in victory celebration chants at camp. At the time, in my mind, the only difference between an Olympic victory lap and a camp victory dance was that the Olympics were viewed by many on television.

I had so much fun creating this wonderful image of my Olympic victory lap. However, my sprint dreams and 4x100m relay victory lap were brought to a halt. One day, after winning the 100-yard dash—during the '70s, the races were measured in yards—at a field day, I told my father that I wanted to be a sprinter. He looked at me with a scoured face and said, "I ran cross country in college and you will run long distances because I want to dispel the notion that American blacks cannot run cross-country and distance." He continued with his long-distance pitch by stating that he was not going to have anyone tell him what his kids could and could not do. I simply stood there listening to him, and I can remember wishing he would be quiet because I knew what he was building up to say, and I did not need to hear anymore. Then finally, I heard him say with a stern matter-of-fact voice, "Your mother and I will make that decision. Distance running builds character, and you have no option." From that point forward, I knew that my 100-yard days were over and I would run the 400m, 800m, mile, and cross-country. The only sprinting that I would do, would be the last 100m of the 800m, mile or distance run. I did not know exactly what my father meant when he said, "Distance running builds character, and you can accomplish whatever you want with parental guidance and discipline." I thought to myself as any seven years old would think, who cares about discipline? However, over the years, many people have committed on my father's thought process regarding distance running; and one person's response was, "I simply think that your father wanted his kids to build a certain kind of character, not simply by avoiding sprinting, but by avoiding a stereotype. Avoiding what he viewed as an 'easier path' by falling into what all of their friends were doing, and what they probably felt was their only track & field-ability based on the tremendous success of other African Americans in sprinting on different levels. I think your father really just wanted you to take the road less traveled in order to build a certain character and prove that with discipline, hard work, support, talent, focus, and zeal, all things are possible. Your father does not want you to avoid sprinting simply because he thinks sprinting can't build tremendous character. He wanted you to take on what would be a greater challenge by going against the grain of things."

In other words he was teaching you about perseverance.

As it turned out, I did not mind training and competing in the distance events. However, at the early age of ten, I am not sure if my minding had any impact on what my father wanted us to do. I say us because my younger brother J. J. also ran middle/distance races. I often felt sorry for him because unlike me, he was really fast and would beat all of the kids he ran against. Even though he was a good sprinter, it would not be long before he too was put into the middle-distance/distance races. As it turned out, we enjoyed training and running through the town, up and down hills and trying to run faster times on many of our courses.

Over time, we won our state meets, national championships; and after twenty-five years, many of our records are still number 1 or the top 10 on several lists. My brother and I both received full athletic scholarships to Villanova University and the University of Tennessee respectively, where our events remained the same.

My sister, Hazel, was born sixteen years after me, and she was constantly trying to avoid the inevitable. Hazel, who is known to us as Peachy, danced, rode horses, ice-skated, and played basketball because she was determined not to run no matter what the distance. However, after trying every sport imaginable, she ran a race at the age of fourteen and won. Can you guess what race she ran? If you said the 800m, you guessed correctly. Hazel too won state competitions, received a full athletic scholarship, and graduated from the University of Florida. Hazel has made three Olympic teams: 2000, 2004, and 2008 at 800m.

Why did I write about how I got started in middle distance? The answer is simple. I thought that it was important to stress the concept of never giving up and how—with direction, drive, and divine intervention—one can accomplish almost any task. Being an athlete has taught me how to be prepared and confident yet humble and thankful for all opportunities and situations. Whether I am delivering a powerful presentation or preparing a proposal, I believe that I can accomplish my goals.

I came to the realization at an early age that if I could run distance and cross-county in the snow, rain, sun, or wind and not give up, I also would not give up when life's situations became challenging for me. It is imperative to understand that the curve in the road is not the end of the road unless you fail to make the turn. Therefore you have to be willing to make the turns as you meander through the curves of life. Always remaining focused on the finish line of accomplishment. The inner drive that was fine turned in sports enabled me to become a better person. It is through sports that I learned regardless of a situation, a champion must fine something in the pit of his/her soul to overcome obstacles.

Over the years, I have been described by others as tough, persistent, stern, serious, loyal, overbearing, direct, funny, humble, and honest. But one thing is sure, win, lose, or draw, I always came to the event prepared and ready to perform. I am thankful for my father's direct action in giving me no options but to run distance and succeed. However, even with all of the support from my parents and life's experiences, nothing prepared me for what was about to happen to me in 1997.

My brother/coach told me that his wife/athlete, Jearl, was going to move up to the 800m and that I would have no option but to train and run against her. After I collected my thoughts and calmed down—and believe me I had to calm down—several thoughts went through my mind: "What do you mean Jearl is moving up? Why! She is doing fine at the 400m? We already have enough competition here. What do you mean I do not have any options? I do too. I can find another coach. Hey, I am your older sister. Why are you doing this? My track career had blossomed after my college days. I was one of the top 800m runners in the USA and the world. I had made two Olympic teams and was poised to continue my reign in the 800m especially in the United States. My brother is no longer an athlete but rather a coach who had developed into one of the best middle distance coaches in the world. He also married Jearl Miles who ran the 400m and had won Olympic gold medals and won the World Championships at that distance, which were great accomplishments, and I was happy for all of her successes. As long as she stayed at the 400m. Believe it or not, to this day, I never asked J. J. any of these questions because in my sane mind I knew it was the right thing for Jearl. She was a 48-second 400m runner with strength, not much quick leg speed. She was getting older and needed to move up to stay in the sport longer, and he wanted what was best for her. But who cares about what is right or wrong for Jearl. It was wrong for me.

And to prove my point, in one of her first European races, she ran an American record at 800m in a time of 1:56.43. Boy did I have a pity party for myself. I could not believe my coach would do this to me, and I went on and on. Until one day, I realized that I did have options. I can mope around, feeling sorry for myself or benefit from the situation. I chose to benefit from the situation by training with her and getting into better shape with my new training partner.

At that time, I had already developed the Joetta *P* principles for success, and this setback would enable me to use the principles as I worked through this maze. So when calmer heads prevailed, I decided to use the first *P*, which is purpose. As I thought about everything, I realized that my purpose in track and field was to be the best that I could be, to win championships, and to leave my mark in the 800m. When my career was over, I wanted my name to be synonymous with the 800 meters. Therefore, in working through this problem, I decided to stay with my brother/coach because he is a great coach; and I said if Jearl is going to set American records, I will too or at least get personal records. But en route to the PRs, there was a defining moment in my career.

In some European races, the meet directors want to have a pacesetter. This person is given splits to hit, and the rest of the athletes sit behind the pacesetter also known as the rabbit. The race rabbit will eventually stop, and the rest of the runners will finish the race, hopefully, in a fast time. I was in Stockholm, Sweden, to run the 800m and I had just run a very fast time and finished third. In the two meets prior and in the Stockholm meet, I watched the rabbit stop in between the 350-meter to 400-meter mark. I was appalled that a rabbit was getting paid and she could not run 56 for the first lap. I thought to myself, *I could run that and keep going.*

After the race, J. J. said that the Zurich meet director wanted me to rabbit the 800m race. He mentioned that the meet director thought that I was the only one that could run the splits for the race. He wanted the first lap to be mid 55 seconds, for me and then run 29 seconds for the next 200m. I should be around 1:24 at the 600m mark. He hoped that the field could finish the last 200m in 30 seconds or faster. I was not excited about that because I wanted to run the race and get a good time too. My coach, J. J., and my new agent, Tony Campbell, left out a bit of information. How much I was going to get paid to be the pacesetter? I did not ask that question, I simply said I will think about it. Later on that day, I said that I would rabbit the race. Then I heard this: "They will pay you $7,000.00 if you run the correct pace to the 500m mark, and if you run the pace of 1:24 seconds for the 600m, you would get $10,000, plus a bonus if the race produces the fastest time in the world. Well, I was confident that I could run the 600m in 1:24 because I had run that in practice with Jearl. I asked them why they had not told me about the price earlier. J. J. answered, "I did not want your decision to be based on money, but it needed to come from the heart in order for you to be committed to the pace." Boy was I committed. I had a great warm-up, and I was excited to be able to pace this race, might I add that I knew that I was not stopping at the 500m. When my coach came over to check on the progress of my warm-up, he said, "How are you doing?" I looked at him and said, "Great." J. J. is my coach, but the next voice I heard was from J. J., my brother, who knew my personality from living with me all of his life. The younger brother whom I had bossed around and gave orders too. The younger brother who was my coach and a well-respected around the world. My brother was 100 percent sure that I was not going to stop at 600m, and when he looked into my eyes, that sparkle confirmed what he already knew. We both knew that I had run 700m, coming through at 600m at 1:24 in practice. I knew I could finish the last 200 in at least 33, which would give me a personal record of 1:57; and just when I began calculating everything, his voice and smirk brought me back to reality. I then heard him say, "Sister"—that is the name that he has called me his entire life—"you have to stop at the 600m mark." I frowned and then smiled and said, "ok."

The race began, and I went to the lead, and to be honest, I never even thought of stopping at the 500m mark. As a matter of fact, when I hit that mark, I ran the last 100m so fast people jokingly commented that it looked like I should have been in the women's open 100m. During my entire time having warm-up, my mind-set was to run the pace and then continue for one hundred more meters to get an additional $3,000.00. Even though I knew that pacesetting was a business, my main objective was to persevere. See, had I given up on myself and my brother/coach, I would not have been in the position to be a rabbit for my sister-in-law/competitor. So often in life, situations that cause us pain and confusion can, in a strange way, provide us with a clarity of purpose. The pain of running long distances, the confusion of "should I stay or should I go," and then the clarity or peace of mind to say, "Weeping may endure for the night, but sunshine will come in the morning." Everyone has a morning, and it comes at different times, but the true winner is the one who is willing to find understanding in the midst of the storm and develop the appreciation to be thankful for their morning.

At the end of the race, everyone was happy. I ran the splits given to me by the meet director. Maria Mutola from Mozambique won the race and set the best time of the year of 1:56.11. The first four athletes ran personal records, and Jearl ran 1:56.43. A couple of meets later, I had the opportunity to run the 800m in Monte Carlo; and I ran 1:57.84, which was a PR for me too.

When my father said I had no option and about twenty years later my brother echoed those same words to me, I was despondent and angry at both of them. However, my love for the 800m allowed me to persevere and become a better athlete and person. In both cases, I could have given up and not received a full scholarship to college and not traveled around the world and not have made a career out of the sport, receiving endorsements from some of the most prominent sports companies, but I chose to be proactive and persevere. In other words, during your life you will face challenges that will make you test your commitment level to your purpose. When this moment comes, you are to remember that success can only be realized when you believe that, *you have no option just keep going.*

Questions:

1. Write about a time in which perseverance was required but you gave up.

   a. Why did you give up?

   b. How did you feel about your decision?

   c. Did you ever go back to complete the task?

2. Describe a current situation in which you are feeling discouraged but you are determined to get your desired outcome.

3. What lesson have you learned about perseverance?

4. If you had to name a chapter about your life in which perseverance was the subject, what would you title the chapter? And why?

5. Think of a time when you had to persevere. Did you accomplish your task alone or were you helped? Who helped you and how did they help?

AFTERWORD

Putting the Ps to Practice

You have covered a lot of material, and you should be proud of yourself. This landmark is something exciting to celebrate as you begin your new journey in life. I have provided you with information that will help you overcome your fears as you take courageous steps toward your victory. I would like to be able to assure you that the road ahead would be straight, but that comment would be untrue. I do, however, want to remind you of these words of wisdom and encouragement the bend in the road is not the end of the road unless you fail to make the turn. I would like to stress the importance of sticking to your plan. It is imperative that you remain flexible during your journey. Remember, be committed to your goal and only apply the brakes to say, "Job well done."

Throughout the chapters, I have shared my stories, my experiences, and my principles, but nothing is more important than painting your own picture of success. It is also important to recognize success and celebrate after your accomplishments. As an Olympian who competed at the highest levels athletically, I can honestly say that I never really celebrated my accomplishments. I was told by parents and coaches not to be boastful and not to display much emotion. These individuals believed that displaying those types of emotions could be interpreted by others as obnoxious. I am certain that many of you share the similar stories regarding acknowledging your accomplishment. Like me, you might have limited yourself from really appreciating or enjoying your accomplishments.

It took over twenty-five years of competing in track and field before I finally was able to appreciate my success. I can vividly remember the day in November 2000 when I decided to put all of my Olympic race numbers in an album. A smile crossed my face as I organized the Olympic race numbers by the years. The first set of race numbers were from the 1988, then 1992, 1996, and 2000. I began to reflect on my career, and I thought about the sacrifices, hard work, discipline, and motivation that enabled me to be an elite athlete. I also thought about the life lessons that I learned from the sport and how I applied them to my life off the track. I thought it was important for me to share this information with you to help you understand how valuable it is for you to congratulate yourself and acknowledge your milestones. It is our human nature to compete and strive to do better and achieve more in life. Since we might feel this way and we are constantly focused on the next task, we fail to appreciate our accomplishments. I believe that it is imperative to celebrate, but in the midst of your you-go-girl or you-go-boy moment, you should exhibit control. It is during this control phase that you are able to accept, evaluate, and navigate to your next celebration.

At the beginning of the book, I said that I would see you at the finish line. My hope is that having now completed this book, you will continue to revisit your goals or obstacles and use the Ps to help you to become a better you. I would like you to select a current area and work through the scenario, applying the Joetta *P* principles to that situation.

1. What is your purpose?

2. How will you prepare?

3. How will you have patience?

4. What will happen when you get perturbed?

5. How will you persevere?

Extra Stories for You

My unedited diary written during the 1996 Summer Olympic Trials and Olympic Games in Atlanta, Georgia.

Competing in the Olympic Games is a goal of every elite athlete. It is a goal I have accomplished three times. This time, however, it will be the experience of a lifetime. I am going to live the dream of all athletes: I will compete in an Olympics in my own country.
I don't know if any of you are able to share my excitement about the games, but I hope that by sharing my experience as an athlete with you through a series of personal diaries, you will understand why these Olympics are so important to athletes.

The following is an insight into my experiences at the Olympic Trials and the weeks leading up to today.

June 12, Atlanta

I arrived on June 12, which was two days prior to the Olympic Trials. In order to make the 1996 Olympic Team, all athletes must compete in this meet. Over the years, track enthusiasts have had many arguments regarding this country's selection process. As it stands now, and will probably remain, the USA's team is chosen based on an athlete's performance at the trials. Some people think athletes should be selected based on their performances over the years. I like the current process. If you want to be on the Olympic team, place in the top three with a qualifying time at the trials.

June 16, Atlanta

My heats went just fine. I advanced through each round quite easily. Most athletes complained about the heat, but I liked the feeling of working up a sweat. The perspiration made me feel like I was getting ready to "take care of business."

One might wonder, what business is she talking about? Well, the business on hand at 7:20 p.m. tomorrow is making my third Olympic team.

June 17, Atlanta

At 7:00 p.m., all of the women 800-meter finalists met under the Olympic Stadium in the holding area. This is the place where I focus on my race strategy. I do spike strides, and I get ready mentally to compete. Not much talking goes on between the competitors. As far as I am concerned, any good luck wishes from my competitors should have been said prior to this point.

Suddenly, I heard a strong voice saying, "Ladies, it's time to walk down."

I grabbed my spikes and walked confidently down the track. OK, I will admit it, my heart was pounding and the 100-yard walk to the starting line seemed like an eternity. All of the competitors had fans screaming for them. However, my supporters appeared to win the shouting match. I usually only hear the voices of family and friends. This time was no different. Or so I thought. Fifty yards from the start, a group of eardrums shattering—but greatly appreciated—fans yelled, "Joetta's in the house. Go! Go! Go!" I usually don't acknowledge outside voices, but something said I would need to hear them toward the end of my race. Moreover, I thought that I had better give them a recognition smile, or they might get louder.

The race went well for me; I crossed the finish line in 1:58.22—nearly a personal record. (My best time is 1:58.06.) After I crossed the finish line, I bent over with a big smile on my face. This expression might have baffled many people because I seldom smile for placing second. However, this smile was one of mixed emotions: (1) I had made the Olympic team and (2) I'll be back to Atlanta in July, representing the United States and going for a gold medal.

I was excited about making the team, and I wanted to share the moment with my loved ones and fans. However, the party would have to wait until I complete the drug testing process. During the test, athletes are required to take, and the pass or fail, results would be revealed about two to three weeks later. By the time I finished the process and arrive to the hotel, much to my surprise, we were met by family members and friends who hugged and kissed me aside from the balloons and flowers that occupied my arms. It was a great feeling seeing the joy on their faces. At that moment, I thought even though I do all the running, the one thing I enjoy is sharing the victory with people.

June 18, Atlanta

I did not get much rest this night because, I guess, I was excited about everything. I say I guess because I am someone who is not easily overcome with emotions. I ate breakfast with my agents at 7:00 a.m. and then went to the USA Olympic congratulations team meeting. I was happy and still running on excitement, but I knew the day before me would be a long one.

We met the Olympic coaches, watched a video, and last but not least, we were sized for our parade and U.S. Olympic uniforms. I had done this before, so I was not that excited. I think my greatest pleasure was watching the first-time Olympians going through this procedure. Most of them looked like kids going through a toy store, smiling ear to ear. My biggest concern was going to a press conference with my family and getting back to finish this procedure. Even though I was in a rush, I did stop to take pictures with the American flag and my uniform. Yeah, you guessed it . . . sentimental reasons.

June 19 to July 15, Europe

I went to Europe to continue to improve on my fitness and work on my race strategy. Sometimes, athletes get so excited about making the Olympic team; they forget about getting ready for the real challenge. My goal was to keep focused, stay healthy, and train harder.

July 16, Gainesville, Florida

Jearl Miles, a world champion and Olympian at 400 meters, and I boarded a 7:00 p.m. Atlanta-bound flight. (By the way, Jearl will also be my sister-in-law, Nov. 30.)

We both had flown this connection many times. However, we agreed this time was different. We were going to pick up our Olympic uniforms and check into the Olympic village. During the flight, we talked about how great it is to have the Olympics in America. For three weeks, Atlanta and the United States will be in the spotlight. I am confident that these Centennial Olympics will be second to none. At 8:00 p.m., the flight arrived on time, and we proceeded to the accreditation area. This is where we pick up our credentials, which allow us access into the Olympic village.

Jearl and I compared pictures and giggled like teenagers. We did not want the other to see "the mug shot." But after we both got the courage to show each other the picture, we agreed that the shows were not too bad. At 10:30 p.m., we are on our way to the Olympic village. En route to the village, we passed a track stadium. A chill ran through my body as I thought, *This is where it happened—me making the Olympic team!*

At 11:00 p.m. we arrived. Even though it was dark, the village was still with light because of the electric ambiance. I could see the other countries' flags and many people socializing. I noticed that there was no line to pick up my house key. I walked over quickly. I wanted to run, but if I did, someone might see my excitement. I picked a room, put my bags down, and looked at my watch: 11:05. Wow, it's late.

The twin-size bed was a little soft, unlike my firm queen-sized bed at home. As I lay on my back looking at the ceiling, I chuckled. Jearl asked, "What's so funny?" I said, "The twin-sized bed is small, but I'd rather be in a small bed in the Olympic village than a big bed at home."

At 11:45 p.m., we turned the lights out.

Cramped Quarters, Spirits High

The first night in the Olympic Village was OK. My dorm room has bunk beds. I prefer sleeping on the bottom bunk because I get up several times during the night. The sleeping quarters are very tight, but the spacious living room/kitchen area makes up for it.

There are eight women to a suite. Jearl (Miles) and I are early risers, and we always make mention of the fact that we do more before 9:00 a.m. than most people do all day.

It is 6:30 a.m. and we are leaving our dorm room to find the cafeteria. We were walking in the direction of the cafeteria when we saw a friend who said, "If you are going to eat, you should hop on the golf cart tram. The place is a mile away from here."

Of course, we hopped on. It always amazes me that I can run eight miles, but I will not walk a mile.

The cafeteria is very large, and at 7:00 a.m. it is quite busy. There is so much food to choose from, and if you are undecided about your entrée, you could stand there all day deciding. I enjoyed watching what people from other countries ate for breakfast. I had cereal, a bran muffin, orange juice, and fruit.

I did not spend much time eating because we had to pick up the rest of our uniform at 9:00 a.m. The trip to Decatur, Georgia, was only twenty minutes, and the line to pick up our equipment wasn't long. We got gifts from all of the sponsors, and I enjoyed everything from our Motorola pagers to the Olympic Cabbage Patch dolls.

It is noon and I am finished. I am on my way to the airport to return to Florida.

At 9:00 p.m., I was unpacking, and I heard that a plane went down en route to Paris. My heart sank, and I said a prayer for the families of the passengers. I could see from the debris in the water that it was a fatal crash. I looked at J. J. (my brother/coach), and he knew from the expression on my face what I was thinking. Eight days ago, I left JFK for Paris. I said another prayer for being alive.

July 18

It is 6:30 a.m. and 85 degrees, and I did a distance run. My training is going along great. I ran five miles. I always did drills and a medicine ball workout for more conditioning. During this phase it is very important not to train too hard. I want to have good workouts but nothing that would make my body sore for days.

I am in great condition. I have to stay in Florida to train in order to become a little sharper for my Olympic races. After my workout, the fun begins. I receive a one-hour sports massage, which is designed to work out the lactic acid and make my muscles relaxed. I emerge from the room as a new athlete.

Since I travel from Gainesville, Florida, to New Jersey quite often, I have to have two sets of therapists. I am very pleased with my New Jersey and Gainesville groups.

At 7:00 p.m., I had lasagna that I made and nice salad. I enjoy cooking, and I think I am pretty good. My parents are excellent cooks, but I think I have surpassed their talents. I do not tell them that because I don't want to be disrespectful, even at this age (just kidding).

July 19

At 8:30 a.m., I had a great interval workout. Everything was faster than my brother and coach J. J. wanted, but it felt effortless. I kept thinking that I am peaking just right. Although it is 90 degrees, the weather did not faze me. I made sure that I drank my Power Gel and I had a PowerBars, which helps me during recovery time.

Tonight is the opening ceremonies. I decided, along with my coach, not to go. I have been involved in two opening ceremonies, and we thought it was best for me to stay home and rest my legs because the ceremonies take about seven hours. We have to get dressed, take team pictures, load the bus, and *all* of the various countries have to get to the holding station where we wait until it is time for us to line up to walk into the stadium by your respective country. Then we have to stand to watch the torch being lit, get back on the bus, and get to the village. So this time I watched the television starting at 8:30 p.m. I watched the energetic dancers, the beautiful colors, and who could forget the children, organized as a dove, that began flying. Everything in the dance had a meaning, and I was interested to hear to commentary.

As we watched the ceremonies, my main concerns were, who did I see on TV? What country would have the straightest line, and who would light the torch?

In 1988, the United States was fined because our group was spread out all over the place. Ever since then, we have been told to stay relatively straight. I think it is important to note that even though you might be overcome with emotions, you must remember you are representing America, so do an excellent job.

It's about 10:00 p.m. and the countries are beginning to march into the stadium lead by that countries' flag bearer. We were looking for our friends and discussed the various uniforms. I remember 1988 and 1992. I wonder when and if I will ever wear my opening uniform again. I actually have a wardrobe that I can wear with the blazer, skirt, and shows. Wow, that is frightening (just kidding again).

What a difference eight years make. It is after midnight, and now the Americans are about to march in. The host country is always last to enter the stadium. Prior to the USA being announced, I discussed that there was only one way to carry the American flag. As I stood up to demonstrate, our flag carrier emerged, holding his right arm straight out in front of him. It was great.

I screamed, clapped, smiled, and yelled, "Here we come!" We started pointing at our friends and laughed at the "I am cool" walks. Considering everything I thought the athletes marched in with a lot of pride and American spirit. Even though I wasn't there, my friends and I felt part of the ceremony.

I am getting tired, but I *must* see the lighting of the torch. I have done so since 1976, and despite feeling exhausted, I had enough energy to stay awake another twenty-five minutes. We were speculating who would light the torch, and boy, were we wrong.

I was really enthused as I watched the torch relay go around the track. Finally, we saw the last person run up the incline, and everyone in the house was perplexed. Before anything was said, a person turned around and it was Ali! We all screamed "ALI! ALI! ALI!" in unison with the people in the stadium

As his strong-looking but shaky physique stood before the world, you could see that he was determined to perform this task with the pride and confidence he displayed as a boxer.

As I watched the fire move slowly toward its destination, I thought, *This will be the "greatest" Olympics, as Ali would say, "of all time!"* At that moment, the torch was lit. What a marvelous sight.

Rundown on the final countdown
July 20

I had no problem getting out of bed at six thirty this morning despite staying up late watching the opening ceremonies. I stretched lightly and then proceeded out into the 80-degree temperature and 100-percent humidity. During my five-mile run, I concentrated on running tall and staying springy.

At this point in my training, it is important to have, in track terminology, "life in the legs." In other words, I do not want to feel as though I am running in quicksand. It is now 9:00 a.m. I am refreshed and hungry. My breakfast consisted of natural oatmeal, a bagel, orange juice, and a glass of water. Later in the day I decided to phone home and retrieve my messages. Although

I was not at the opening ceremonies, I was confident some of my friends would say that they saw me. Of course, I was right. Three people said they saw me on TV, and they taped the event. I called Kevin (my former training partner) and told him he did not see me because I was in Gainesville. Do you know what his response was? "Are you sure?" After listening to him describe the event and the people he saw me walking with, he had me convinced that I was in Atlanta.

Later that evening I watched the Olympics and the enthusiastic American crowds made me want to compete now. I watched the Dream Team, but when I saw that the opposing team was close to them at halftime, I lost interest and went to sleep.

July 21

I had a late practice today which enabled me to watch swimming and some of the other events. Sometimes it is very hard for me to watch the games because I become so excited. Whenever I watch the Olympics, my heart palpitates because I imagine myself competing. The determination and the guts that the athletes displayed reminds me of the fortitude that I will have to display in five days. Regardless of the number of meets I compete in, I still get nervous. But I like to think of it as good feeling instead of a nervous because I did not put the work in. A nervous feeling creates anxiety and an inability to compete effectively.

July 22

At 7:30 a.m., I was on my way to practice, and I was already drenched in sweat. I had an excellent workout, which consisted of 1x600, 1x400, 1x300 and 2x200 strides and drills. Most of the intervals were done at race pace. I also tried to visualize different parts of my race. My goal is to run as aggressively but relaxed as I can at the Olympics. It is also important that I stay in contact with my competitors. After I got my much-needed massage, I submerged my reluctant body into an ice bath for ten minutes. The rest of my day consisted of packing my bags to return to the Olympic village.

July 23

I had a different kind of workout today. I usually run to the track, which is five miles. However today J. J. (my coach) wanted me to walk a mile, run three miles, and walk another mile. It was 6:45 a.m. and I started with my workout. I was hesitant about walking because I did not want anyone to see me walking. Many people exercise by walking, "power walking," and with my competition quickly approaching, I felt uncomfortable walking on the streets. I did not want anyone to think that I was "power walking"; therefore, I tried not to bounce my head and over swing my arms. It appeared that it was taking an eternity just to walk a mile. When I finally finished my workout, the smile on J. J.'s face ended all my fears. Someone had seen me and told him I was walking. Unknown to them, walking was part of the workout.

J. J. said, "One of the trainers said they saw you walking. Moreover, they were surprised because they had never seen you walking." What I wanted to know was, if they had never seen me walking, why didn't they stop and see if I was OK?

It is 5:00 p.m. and I am at the village going through "gender testing." During this procedure, a piece of hair is plucked from the roots, and the inside of your jaw is scraped. This test is supposed to verify your gender.

At 8:00 p.m., the village is very active. I tried to find some of my friends, but everyone went to a concert in the village to hear Monica, an R&B singer, perform. I walked around the blue zone, where the USA is housed, and talked to some water polo and weight lifting athletes. At 10:30 p.m., lights out.

July 24

The countdown has begun for me. In two days, my first round will be over. Even though my focus is becoming more intense, I did not want to be overwhelmed by this feeling. Subsequently, I went downtown on the Marta, a subway, and it was crowded but orderly. Peachtree Street is closed to traffic, and people are everywhere. Everyone is friendly and interested in knowing your hometown. I signed autographs and took pictures with appreciative tourists. When I had my quiet time today, I thought about how thankful I am to be able to compete in my third Olympics. However, I was more overcome with the thought of how I have made my family, friends, and fans proud of me. I am so appreciative of their support.

July 25

"THEY'RE HERE!"

My family and friends made their presence felt as they took Atlanta by storm. Even though I was happy to see them, I had to remain calm. I have my first heat tomorrow, and it was important for me to get stretched, have a massage, and stay off my feet. I am very excited about my run tomorrow, and my goal is to advance to the next round. I know that I am in the best shape of my life; now it is my time to represent the USA.

Before I went to sleep, J. J. (coach) gave me a preparation talk, and then J. J. (brother) gave me a hug. J. J. is my coach/brother. As my high school coach, Mr. Klepack, would say, "GO GET THEM, JO!"

In midst of a painful defeat, a reason to be thankful
July 26

At 7:30 a.m., I got dressed and went to eat breakfast. I had hot cereal, a muffin, fruit salad, and orange juice. After that, I went for my pre-race walk to get a bit of fresh air. The streets of Atlanta were not too crowded at that time, but I could feel the electricity building on Peachtree Avenue.

I did some light stretching in the room at 9:30 and thought about my race strategy. My goal today was to stay in contact with the leaders, cover moves, allow no gaps between myself and the competition, and have a kick the last one hundred meters.

At noon, I started to put on my uniform. I usually compete in a half-top, but I decided not to this time. Had I done so, the "USA" on my uniform would have been covered by my race number, and it was important for me to have the "USA" visible.

The U.S. coach wanted to meet me at the bus in the village at 2:00 p.m., and I was there on time. When I arrived at the warm-up track, I was met by J. J. (coach/brother), who already reserved a quiet spot under a tent for me. I felt relaxed, and I was confident that I would execute the strategies that we worked on in practice.

I began my warm-up at 3:20 p.m., which gave me plenty of time. My warm-up went great. I felt good when I did my sprints, and I did all of my pre-race drills.

J. J. was carefully watching over me to make sure everything was going smoothly. It was now 4:30 p.m., and the last call for the women's 800 meter was made. It was time to go. The ride with my competitors over to the stadium was a quiet one. Everyone had their game faces on, myself included. I was in the fourth heat, and as I waited for my turn, I watched the other heats. There was a call for my heat, and I walked confidently to my position. As

I entered the stadium, people were calling my name and waving the American flag. The next thing I heard was the command, "Runners set," and then the gun. I got out well, and I was going to take position on the leader's shoulder, but instead she moved to the outside of lane 1 and allowed me to take the inside position. In previous races, I slowed down before 400 meters, which allowed everyone to pass me, but not this time. As Anna Quiriot (Cuba) tried to go by, I picked up. I ran comfortably but aggressively down the backstretch and was in the lead. I had done everything right for 600 meters.

My competitors tried to go by with 150 meters left, but I effortlessly held them off. With 100 meters left, I was in front with Anna next to me, as she had been during the entire race. I started my kick. We went back and forth, she edged in front a little, and then I reacted to another runner who was also in full pursuit. I went to my arms, digging and covering her moves. I had done everything right; my arm movement was short and quick, and I gave it everything I had. But when I crossed the finish line in third place, it took all of my resolve not to fall to the track. I took a quick glance at the time and saw 1:59.9, and I knew that my Olympic quest to make the finals was over. Only the top two in each heat, plus the next six fastest times made it back to the semifinals. As I dejectedly walked off the track, I replayed the race in my head. Under the stadium, I saw reporters whom I acknowledged with eye contact. I hoped that they would not ask me any questions, so I asked them the first question, "Did my time get in?" They answered in unison, "I do not think so."

I quickly got dressed so I could meet J. J. at the practice track as scheduled. However, before I could leave the stadium, a couple of reporters stopped me. I would have answered most of their questions under normal circumstances, but after about ten minutes, I said, "Fellas, I am going to cut this short. Thank you." When I arrived at the warm-up track, I did not want to speak to anyone.

I spotted J. J., who walked over and gave me a hug. Before he could speak, I said in a sobbing voice, "What happened?" His response was that, "You just got beat." He began to talk, I sniffled, he talked, I wiped a tear. He stopped talking and said for me to jog down. I took some deep breaths and jogged around the track. I took my Killer Loop glasses off as I jogged to show J. J. that I would regroup and pull myself together. Win, lose, or draw, I never want my competitors to see me sweat or, in this case, shed an unfamiliar tear.

The ride back in a van with J. J. was peaceful. He mentioned that I had done everything right. He thought that I had finally put a race together. He also said that I did not give up, and I am in the best shape of my life. At that time, I wanted to ask, "Then why am I not in the semifinals?" However, I nodded and looked out of the window until we arrived at the hotel. I was greeted with hugs from my mother, sister, aunt, and boyfriend. We all had dinner.

I prepared for sleep just after midnight, but I remembered this, "Faith is believing in the absence of success. Do not lose hope in my dream it has not been completed yet, it is only delayed."

July 27

I was up at 6:00 a.m. I reached for my pager to see if I had any "pity messages." It was good I did not have any. My friends knew not to do that to me. As I scrolled down the few keep-your-chin-up messages, I read that a pipe bomb exploded, killing and injuring people.

I popped out of bed, said a quick prayer for everyone, and turned in the news. As I watched the news, I became more and more outraged. In just two weeks, the lives of more innocent people were destroyed because of a bomb.

We ventured out in the streets of Atlanta, and the amount of enforcement officers was clearly visible. Security all around the hotels and the village had increased. The mood in the hotel was different from the mood in the village. People in the hotel told stories about being at Centennial Park that morning or having previously stood in the spot where the bomb exploded. The athletes showed emotions from tears to expressing that they wanted to leave Atlanta.

I think the city and the volunteers have tried their best to welcome the world to the Olympics. It is a travesty to have this event, or any event, marred by terrorism. Around 6:15 p.m., we were returning from the Olympic village. We got off the MARTA in the underground area and heard people say that there was a bomb threat in the underground, which was quickly closed. We started to walk toward Marietta Street and started hearing more and more ambulances. All of a sudden, thousands upon thousands of people began walking our way.

Police began roping off the area and sending traffic out of the area. People were calm, but frustrated because they were not told what or where to go.

I knew where I was going; I was going back to my hotel.

At 7:00 p.m., I got a page from a friend that stated that the track meet was pushed back. When we got back to the hotel lobby, we asked what had happened. The person said that there were bomb threats at the underground that forced them to close some lines of the MARTA. We all looked at each other; and as I was about to say that I was going upstairs, they said, "I am hungry and I am going outside to eat. I am not going to let this news take away my Olympic spirit."

Even though I did not want to go back outside, I was with friends and walked back outside with them to get some dinner.

We all had a peaceful dinner. Before I went to sleep, I said a prayer for the families of the victims. I also thought that even though I did not make the semifinals, life goes on. I am thankful to be alive another day.

July 28
Looking back, my Olympic experience was solid gold all the way.

My day began at 8:00 a.m. with a small breakfast with friends. I was not very hungry, but they wanted to take me out, so I went with them. After breakfast, I visited another friend in Decatur, Georgia.

I enjoyed staying around friends because it took my mind off my race. However, there were times when I thought about my race and not being in the finals. Around 5:00 p.m., we were off to watch the Dream Team play. Although I am a basketball fan, this time I was not too excited; but we got tickets for the game, so I went. Of course, the game was a blowout. I think the most exciting moment occurred when Dennis Rodman strolled down the aisle with three minutes left in the game. It was so wild; everyone in the dome stood up and cheered as he walked in. For about one minute, absolutely, no one paid attention to the game; all eyes and cameras were on Dennis.

After the game, I traded pins with people from the USA and other countries. I was amazed with the pin collections some people possessed. I enjoyed my day, and I was glad to get out and socialize with people.

July 29

I took my mother and friend to the athletes village today. At 11:00 a.m., we were on the campus of Georgia Tech, and they were taking picture after picture. The campus is so widespread that we had to see the sights by tram. As we toured the village, I could see a difference in the athletes' demeanor. This time, athletes were trading uniforms, eating with people from other countries, and socializing in the International Zone.

The International Zone is where games, shows, and other entertainment are located. I played Q-zar Laser Tag, which is a game that all the athletes talked about in the village. It is a laser tag game played by two or more teams. You score points by shooting a laser beam at opponents as they move through a maze. Usually, I wouldn't play a game that requires running; but since I did not make the finals, I did not have to stay off my legs. My guests had a great time in the village.

Around 5:00 p.m., I found myself at the Olympic Stadium. Even though I sat in nosebleed seats, the view was very good. Around 7:30, the final round of the women's 800 meters was about to begin. We were trying to pick the winner. It was difficult to watch this race from the stands because I had beaten these athletes before.

I watched the race in disbelief as they ran at a pedestrian pace. My heart raced as though I were out there competing. At that time, I knew in my heart that if I had been in the race, I would have executed my plan. As they finished in a slow time of 1:58, I looked at my friend and said, "I just ran 1:58.22 on this track in the Olympic Trials."

I think I enjoyed the meet more after the 800 was over. I watched Jearl (my brother's fiancée) run her best time of 49.5 for the 400m, which was only good for fifth place. I watched Michael Johnson destroy a field of four hundred runners and Carl Lewis win the long jump. I wanted to stay longer, but we left early to beat the MARTA traffic. Unfortunately, everyone else had the same idea. I got home at midnight.

July 30

Today was a rest day for track and field. It was also my rest day. I had walked all over Atlanta, and I wanted to allow my legs to recover. After all, I still have to compete in Europe. I met with Brian (my agent) and J. J. (my coach), and we discussed my European track season. I have been running in Europe since 1981, and I have never missed a season. I enjoyed the traveling, the racing, and the other benefits of running in Europe. As I listened to them talk, it occurred to me that I had not run in three days. After the meeting, I went for a four-mile run. Afterward, I stretched and completed a few drills and motivated myself for my next competitions.

July 31

At 7:00 a.m., I found myself instinctively putting on my polar heart monitor as I got ready for a run. I was not surprised that once I started training again, my enthusiasm for the sport had not diminished. During my run, I continued to monitor my heartbeat to ensure that I did not run too hard. I kept telling myself that I was in good shape but I just did not make the finals. During the off-season, I give motivational speeches, and I often talk about something I call SCAGES—sacrifices, commitment, attitude, goals, enthusiasm, and support. Today, I was giving this speech to myself.

I had set goals for myself in this sport, and I had not reached them. I believed that I could have achieved so much more this season, but my current goal is to redeem myself. I believe that it is important for everyone to leave behind a legacy, in every aspect of their lives. As I go to Europe to compete, I want to continue to work on my track legacy.

August 1

Today is my birthday. My sister tried to keep me up until midnight so I could be awake the minute 12:00 a.m. rolled around. However, my objective was to get rest so I could catch my early-morning flight. I decided not to stay in Atlanta for the closing ceremonies because I did not want to tackle the long lines that would inevitably start in the village.

I know from experience that I would have to leave the village four hours prior to my 8:00 a.m. flight. As I checked in, people stopped me to say that they had seen me run and how proud they were of me. I smiled and thanked everyone. On my flight, I thought about my experience and what I had learned. I was even more convinced that age is irrelevant with Carl Lewis's victory and Mary Ellen Clark's comeback. I felt blessed to be alive and healthy as I prepared to land at Newark Airport.

I remembered watching the high-energy opening ceremonies and Muhammad Ali lighting the torch. I thought about my disappointment, along with Janet Evans's and Jackie Joyner Kersee's in the heptathlon. I smiled when I thought about the support I received from my mother, father, siblings, and friends. However, the smile was short-lived when I remembered the bomb in Centennial Park that had killed and injured innocent people.

After reviewing the 1996 Olympics, I think the city of Atlanta and the American people embraced these games. I arrived home to several messages, birthday flowers, and cards. I even received a phone call from the Nelson family, who sang their family version of "Happy Birthday." Around 5:00 p.m., I began to unpack. As I unpacked, I thought about running at Weequahic Park, training for age-group competitions, running at Columbia High

School, continuing at the University of Tennessee, competing for Footlocker, and making every USA team since 1985, and I smiled. Then a thought came to my mind, *I never received any gold medal in the Olympics, but I received the gold medal of life.* Besides, there is always the 1997 World Championships in Athens, Greece. See you there.

My unedited diary written during the 2000 Summer Olympic Trials and Olympic Games 2000

September 17

Today was the first day that I was able to have a full breakfast in the village cafeteria because my practice session was in the afternoon.

Therefore, at 8:00 a.m., Connie Price-Smith, a shot-putter, and I went to the International Zone where we had pancakes that were made-to-order. I ate five well-done pancakes with fruit and apple juice. We ate entirely too much and ended up sitting and looking at people for about an hour. Seating in the area is limited, and as Connie left, a guy asked if he could sit in her seat. He was from Cameroon, which is a country on the upper west side of Africa. Abdul is twenty-nine years old, and he runs the 200 meters. His native tongue is French, but he could speak some English. I took French in high school and have learned enough to piece some words together. So picture this: two people speaking terrible English and French to each other. We communicated this way for about fifteen minutes.

The atmosphere in the village is different now because the competition has started. The home team is doing very well in the swimming pool, and the news station wants everyone to know about it. It appears weird to watch coverage of the games by Australian TV because the coverage appears to focus primarily on swimming. The broadcasters are very excited with their team's performances, and listening to the commentary, one would think that every competing Australian athlete has just won a medal.

While watching the games on TV or seeing athletes returning from their competitions, I think about my race. I look at the courage these athletes are displaying and the medals being won, and I think about what I must do to perform my best.

I had another solid workout that consisted of 3x300 meters and 4x100 meters, stretching, and drills. At this point, most of the work has been done, and I just want to feel quick and relaxed. I have not seen many of my competitors yet, but they should start showing up soon. The more competitors I see, the more I think about beating them. Their appearance allows me to mentally prepare myself for the race.

The day went by quickly, and I attribute that to the much-anticipated arrival of my husband and my family. I have not seen them for about five weeks. I call home and e-mail them, but that does not replace being with them.

September 18

I was up at 5:00 a.m., catching a bus to the airport to meet my husband, Ronald. The flight was on time, and he arrived at 7:00 a.m. It felt really good to be out of the village and around non-athletes. I have been in the village so long, I have forgotten that the town of Sydney existed. After settling down, we took a train to Circular Quay, which is where the famous Opera House, Sydney Harbour Bridge, the AMP Tower, and other landmarks are. I do not like walking around too much prior to competition, so I did not go inside each location. However, after my finals, we will have plenty of time to see the sights.

September 19

Today was the first time that I got a little nervous about my competition. I kept thinking that in three days, I would run in my fourth Olympics. I tried to remain calm by using the positive thought process, and I began feeling better. I spent most of my day relaxing.

After dining, we noticed that the temperature had dropped about 10 degrees. The weather here has been unseasonably warm, and I am hopeful that it will continue through the games. The highs are around seventy-eight degrees, and the lows are about fifty-five to sixty degrees. My first race is in the morning.

September 20

My mother and my aunt arrived safely to their hotel this morning. They seemed happy to be in Sydney and at the Olympic Games. I was happy to see them and hear the excitement in their voices. My father was unable to make the trip, and for some reason, I kept thinking that he is going to show up. I stayed with them for about one hour, and then I headed back to the village for my pre-race isolation. I jogged, stretched, and got a massage; after which, I went to look at my heats for the race on Friday.

September 21

One more day before my show starts. I got the heats; and Jearl is in heat 2, I am in heat 3, and Hazel is in heat 4. We all have tough heats, but on paper, my heat is the toughest. My heat could be considered the toughest because the athletes in my heat have run faster times than the others. There is a system that the Olympic committee uses, which tries to separate athletes based on time. However, with more than forty women entered in a race, some fast people will wind up in the same heat. I rested most of the day and focused on my race strategy. It is important for me to stay close to the pack and stay out of boxes with 200 meters left. Even though I have a good finishing kick, in the Olympics, I will have a hard time passing people if I am off the pace. My warm-up consisted of stretching, massage, and chiropractic adjustments.

Prior to Ronald leaving the village, he reminded me how special I was for being at the Olympics with my family.

Opening ceremonies, a moving experience

Last Saturday was different from my other days in the Olympic village because I knew exactly where I was going. The layout of the village is simple, but at night, it appears complicated. There is the main street that runs up and down the village that they call the artery. This is the street that the buses and cars travel. The cafeteria is about eight hundred meters from my house, and I find myself walking that distance most of the time. There is an international section where athletes can mingle, watch movies, shop, get haircuts, and listen to different musical shows. This is also the place where athletes meet their family members to bring them into the village. The practice tracks are just a bus ride away.

One day, on my way to the practice track, I asked the bus driver about the Olympic village. He said that the area now known as Newington was once a waste dump. He also said that old weapons from World War II were stored underground at this site. When I heard his narrative, I thought he was joking and laughed. I then confirmed his story. The village is a new development site, which sits on about ninety acres of land. Our village is fenced in and heavily guarded. The people I have spoken to agree that the police presence is not threatening. We all have coded badges that the guards examine with decoding guns that validate the credential. I am familiar with the process from previous Olympic Games, and it is very effective.

My coach has a credential that gives him access to the practice track. It is very important for J. J. (Clark) to administer and oversee our practices at this time. He can watch our sessions and make the necessary adjustments. His presence ensures that we do not train too hard. Oftentimes, athletes try to impress their competitors, who happen to practice at the track, by doing meaningless workouts. I just want to stay healthy and calm because I know that I am in good condition.

Sunday morning was hectic because many athletes had early practice sessions, allowing them to get ready for the opening ceremonies. Around 4:00 p.m., the United States athletes began to assemble at our position. This is always a fun time because we have the opportunity to meet U.S. athletes from other sports and take pictures. I felt like a celebrity because everyone wanted to take a picture with the Team Captain and with Team Clark.

Finally, the moment we had been waiting for arrived. "Will the USA team please stand." We all stood up and were directed into the hallway. Since the countries march in alphabetical order, we were one of the last teams out. They organized us by flag bearer, team captains, women, and men.

As we entered the stadium, it was a magnificent feeling. Flags were waving, people screaming, and I was smiling ear to ear. Even though I had done this before, I was just as excited and energized. As we walked into the infield and waited for Australia to walk in, I keep looking at the beautiful stadium and thinking, *The same amount of people will be here on Friday to see me run.* I was overwhelmed and quickly changed my thoughts back to this breathtaking moment.

As we waited for the torch to make it to the stadium, I talked to people, and we tried to guess who would bring the torch in. Our guess was correct, but we did not figure out how the flame would be lighted. When the torch was brought around and the announcer mentioned that these games were in celebration of women, I thought that was wonderful. I clapped and took pictures as the true Australian crusaders of many sports went around the track. At that moment, I was proud to see those women being honored—many sixty years of age.

The lighting of the flame was one of the most spectacular sights I have witnessed. As Kathy Freeman bend over to light the flame in the water, the crowd—and I—erupted. The waterfall and the lighting made Kathy look larger than life. When she walked out of the waterfall and through the water, it was very special for her and the country. After the beautiful ceremony, the pandemonium began, because all of the athletes have to exit out of one entrance and race back to catch a bus.

On Saturday, I was up early again, and I managed to do a slow run. However, the rest of the day, I did nothing. I was very tired and had a hard time walking up and down the steps. I took a bus to the International Zone and listened to groups play music for about four hours. I talked to people a little, but this is the one time that I wanted to be alone and enjoy my Olympic experience and my Olympic peacefulness.

September 22
"Track has been good to me"

After breakfast, I got dressed for my first round. While putting on my uniform, a prideful feeling consumed my spirits. I felt really fortunate to be an American and to have my family members on the team with me.

Prior to leaving the room, I checked to see if I had my spikes, my water bottle, and my running shades. After that was done, I had about ten minutes to collect my thoughts. I walked alone to the bus and met J. J., Jearl, and Hazel. We took the 7:00 a.m. bus over to the practice stadium. The ride was different today because people were not as talkative as usual, and the competing athletes had on their team uniforms.

We arrived at the warm-up track, and Team Clark set up our spot over by the USA trainers. Then we went inside because it was still only fifty-four degrees. I was hopeful that by race time, the temperature would reach its regular high of seventy.

My warm-up went well, and I felt ready for my first round. Before going into the call room, J. J. reminded me that only two from each heat, plus the next six fastest times, advance to the semifinals. Jearl was in the heat before me, and I watched her win in 2:01.79. I was in the next heat, and I took fourth in 2:00.19. The winner of my heat ran 1:59.60. So after my heat, I had the second fastest time, and the third person in my heat had the fastest non-qualifying time of 2:00.18. I watched Hazel take second in her heat of 2:01.99. I anxiously watched the final heat and hoped it was not very fast. As it turned out, I advanced to the semifinals on time. During my warm down, I analyzed my race and mentally prepared myself to run a better, more aggressive semifinal.

As I sat down outside the warm-up area, which is about two hundred yards from the main stadium, I could hear the crowd cheering for the athletes. The stadium seats about 115,000 people and was filled to capacity. My family sat in the upper section, and they had a difficult time seeing my race. My husband said that he would bring binoculars for tomorrow's events. Some of the other athletes' parents mentioned that they would do the same.

The final selection was different from my other teams. In previous years, the top 4 advance to the finals; however, this year, the top 3 plus the next two fastest times advance. Regardless of the situation, I will have to run my best race of the season.

September 23

I slept in this morning because my semifinal race was at 7:00 p.m. Therefore, I went to eat breakfast around 9:30 a.m. After my meal, I walked to the training room and got my pre-race massage. We have a staff of therapists and doctors who were selected by the United States Olympic Committee. The medical staff consists of about twenty people, and they have to treat the entire USA team.

As I got dressed for my competition, I was calm and confident about my race strategy. I knew that I would have to run my season's best time to advance, and I was ready to do that. I met J. J. at the bus stop at 4:00 p.m. Then we all went to the warm-up stadium. The weather was warm and sunny at that time, but I knew by race time, it would be at least ten degrees cooler. My warm-up went well, and I really liked my striders. I was in the second heat with my sister and Jearl was in the first heat. When I heard the final call for my race, I began to get nervous. It was a positive feeling, which lets me know I am at a race, not practice. I wished Hazel well and went into the call room. I watched Jearl run and not qualify for the finals. I was disappointed for her, but my focus quickly went back to me. The next thing I remember hearing was the start's voice saying, "Runners set," and the gun was fired.

I was in lane 8, and I knew that I had to go out fast to get into position. However, after 200 meters, I was in the back of the pack, and things did not get much better during the race. I was never in the race, and I really do not know why. I suppose that I thought the race was fast, and I would run my pace until the girls came back to me. However, I ended up in last place. After the race I, did not have any emotions one way or the other. My concern at that point was looking at the times to see if Hazel advanced. When the times came up on the scoreboard, I told her she made it. Hazel was happy, and I was pleased that she was in the finals.

Prior to leaving the stadium, I did some interviews and confirmed the race was my last. I really did not want my season to end with me running such a poor race, but that is exactly what happened. When I finally reached J. J., he gave me a brotherly hug.

Then he put on his coach's hat on and said that I never gave myself a chance. I offered no excuses, and we went over my training and how inconsistent I was because of my car accident. In 1998, I had a serious car accident and was not able to train for about three months. My car was hit by a 18 wheeler truck and as a result I was hospitalized and sustained head, back, neck, leg, oblique and other injuries. These injuries were serious and my every thought focused on me walking and being able to move pain free. Even though J. J. said that the very fact of me running again was truly a remarkable comeback. He would have like to see me perform better and run tough against the girls. He also said that my enthusiasm level was different after the accident, and that was the edge that I had over the years. I agreed with him.

During our coach/athlete conversation, he said something that summed it all up in a nutshell. "Joetta, you trained out of habit, but not with purpose." He continued with other things and finally said, "What is most important is I did not hear you make any excuses, and that is the sign of a true champion."

For some reason, I did not have any emotion. I kept waiting for this big flow of tears, but tears never came. Instead, I had a clear head, and I told myself that I am prepared to move forward. Then I smiled and said, "Track has been good to me."

September 25

I went to the track around 6:00 p.m. and got caught up in the excitement of Cathy Freeman, the Australian 400-meter runner. The next event that I had the most interest in was my sister's 800-meter race.

During Hazel's warm-up, I got very nervous. It felt as if I was getting ready to run. I watched the warm-up with J. J., and we agreed that she looked focused and fluid. I wished her luck, and then I went into the stadium.

The gun went off, and Hazel was out in front. I thought that she was in great position because the other girls were not pushing her around. When the race was over, she finished in seventh place with a personal record. I was very proud of her performance, and J. J. was too. We both thought that she put herself in position to win the race. For a quick moment, I thought how exciting that would have been.

However, Hazel has more opportunities to make other championship finals. Moreover, Team Clark is still alive because Jearl and Hazel will make many more teams together.

Good-bye to Sydney, Olympic Career

During one of my sleepless nights in Sydney, I decided to do some writing. I plugged in my laptop, and much to my dismay, my computer would not come on. I pushed the button harder and waited for something to happen. Nothing happened again. I wanted to throw the laptop out of the window. So at 3:00 a.m., during my creative moment, I could not type my thoughts, I had to document my thoughts on paper with pencil and pen.

I wrote about thirty pages before I finally stopped to check the time. It was about 6:30 a.m., and my hand was cramping. I tried to power up my computer, but still nothing happened. Therefore, I wrote a note to two of my housemates. One had a Toshiba laptop with DVD, and my friend Sharon Couch, a 1992 Olympian in the long jump and 2000 Olympian in the hurdles, had a Dell/DVD system. My note read as follows: "Help! My laptop is broken, my hand is tired. Can I borrow your computer?" Signed, "Team Captain, Joetta Clark Diggs." The next day Sharon typed as I dictated my diary. Wow, what a friend and what team work.

For our one-year anniversary, Ronald and I saw the sights at Darling Harbor, the Opera House, the Rocks District, and we went to the Waterfront Restaurant for dinner. The ambiance was peaceful, and the food was delicious. We also had a wonderful view of the Harbour Bridge that had Olympic rings made up of white lights hanging from the center of the bridge. It was truly a spectacular and memorable site.

While I packed my bags for my departure from the Sydney 2000 Olympics, I had the opportunity to briefly reminisce about my humble beginnings in Weequahic Park in Newark, New Jersey. I quickly realized how much I had accomplished. I thought about how fortunate I was to have Mr. Kelpack as my high school coach while at Columbia High School. Many coaches would have burned out their athletes, but that did not happen to me, giving me more room to develop. I also realized that after four Olympic teams, I had never won a gold medal. However, I believe that I won the gold medal of life. I received an education from the University of Tennessee, I traveled around the world, I became independent, I met an array of people, and most of all, I learned skills and characteristics that are needed to be successful in life.

Prior to leaving the village, coaches and athletes commended me on my career. I graciously accepted their complements and wished them well in the future. For some reason, I was not frustrated with my track career. Instead, I was excited about my future sports/business ambitions. During this season, my focus was to compete and represent my country in a positive fashion. Moreover, I always wanted to leave the sport under my own volition, and I accomplished that.

The general consensus in Sydney is that the 2000 Olympics was very organized and the spectators were enthusiastic about the games. As always, it takes all types of individuals to make an event successful. Moreover, I believe that a couple of motivated people can help make someone's dream a reality. Therefore, I am grateful for the support Ronald and I received during the games.

Ronald and I left the Olympics prior to the closing ceremonies to avoid the athletes' village and airport mayhem. There were a couple of medalists on the airplane, and they proudly walked around the plane displaying their medals. People clapped, cheered, and wanted to touch the gold medals; and the pilot even recognized their accomplishments. I thought to myself, *How exciting it must be to have a gold medal or any Olympic medal.* Even thought, I did not have a medal to show. I did wear my USA team issued uniform back home and that was a proud moment for me. The USA did not completely dominate the games, and this transition of changing of the guard is necessary to ensure greater success in the future. I told my sister that I was the last American at 800 meters to make the Olympic finals since 1992. Hazel finished seventh in this Olympics and will have more opportunities to place higher.

I arrived home after being away for more than six weeks. I dreaded going through the mail and unpacking my bags. However, I reminded myself that my season is over, and I had plenty of time to organize everything. I carefully took my Olympic bib numbers out of the bag and placed it with my other Olympic numbers. It was then, for the first time, that I felt emotional. When I saw my Seoul, Barcelona, Atlanta, and Sydney numbers together, I was overwhelmed with a great deal of pride. I thought to myself, "I am a four-time Olympian," and said, "Job well done!" Most of my career, I was so concerned with getting better that I forgot to recognize my talent and appreciate my accomplishments. I would like to thank everyone for the opportunity to share my Olympic experiences. I thank my husband for making the trip to Sydney. To my brother/coach J. J., his patience and coaching prowess which are second to none. His track record indicates that he is one of the best elite-conditioning coaches in the world. To Hazel and

Jearl, I thank them for making Team Clark synonymous with the women's 800 meters. I thank my fans, family, and sports medical staff for encouraging me over the years. And finally, I thank my mother and father for always taking the time to be exemplary parents. They never once wavered on making the necessary sacrifices in their lives to prepare me for the opportunities in my life.

I have enjoyed writing this diary, and I anxiously await my book. However, in the meantime, I will continue with my motivational speaking / sports wellness business, Joetta Sports & Beyond, and working with kids on the grassroots level.

Hazel, Jearl, and J. J. developed a saying for my last year of competition—"The lane is empty." That statement is true, and there are many memories from that lane.

Thank you all for being the wind beneath my wings. Keep soaring.

Quotes for Inspiration

The Joetta P Principles for Success is a book intended to provide guidance and inspiration. During my life, I constantly use my P's to help navigate through my every day occurrences. I have also discovered the importance of reading, understanding and applying quotes to my life. I believe that the P's coupled with various quotes have given me the direction, peace and strength to challenge and appreciate my existence. I would like to share some quotes and sayings with you that I have found useful in my life. The following words of wisdom have challenged me to tap into my inner most feelings in order to understand the very essence of the words. By understanding the power behind the words you will immediately realize the power within you.

In this section of the book carefully read the quotes and write what you think is important about the quote as it relates to moments in your life. It is imperative that you take your time to fully understand the words and the overall concept of the saying because you are worth every minute. I would also like you to write an instance in your life that relates to the quotes listed below. There are pages after the quotes that have been designated for you to develop your inspirational quotes. I encourage you to be creative as you write your quotes for inspiration and who knows your quotes just might inspire you and others to achieve greatness and peace. Readers Set! Go!

"If you don't like something, change it. If you can't change it, change your attitude."
Maya Angelou

_____

_____

_____

_____

Quotes for Inspiration

"Our deepest fear is not that we are inadequate. Our deepest fear is that we are powerful beyond measure. It is our light, not our darkness, that most frightens us. Your playing small does not serve the world. There is nothing enlightened about shrinking so that other people won't feel insecure around you. We are all meant to shine as children do. It's not just in some of us; it is in everyone. And as we let our own lights shine, we unconsciously give other people permission to do the same. As we are liberated from our own fear, our presence automatically liberates others."
Nelson Mandela

_____

_____

_____

_____

_____

_____

_____

"What lies behind us and what lies before us are tiny matters compared to what lies within us."
Ralph Waldo Emerson

_____

_____

_____

_____

_____

_____

_____

_____

Quotes for Inspiration

"Preparation is important, and we must be fearless as we prepare for the success and riches that await us."
Joetta Clark Diggs

_____

_____

_____

_____

_____

_____

"It's a lack of faith that makes people afraid of meeting challenges and I believe in myself."
Mohammed Ali

_____

_____

_____

_____

_____

_____

"The greatest danger for most of us is not that our aim is too high and we miss it, but that it is too low and we reach it."
Michelangelo

_____

_____

_____

_____

Quotes for Inspiration

"There is always something to do. There are hungry people to feed, naked people to clothe, sick people to comfort and make well. And while I don't expect you to save the world I do think it's not asking too much for you to love those with whom you sleep, share the happiness of those whom you call friend, engage those among you who are visionary and remove from your life those who offer you depression, despair and disrespect."
Nikki Giovanni

_____
_____
_____
_____
_____
_____
_____
_____
_____

"Friends... they cherish one another's hopes. They are kind to one another's dreams."
Henry David Thoreau

_____
_____
_____
_____
_____
_____
_____
_____

Quotes for Inspiration

"Any man's finest hour, the greatest fulfillment of all that he holds dear is the moment when he has worked his heart out in a good cause, and lies exhausted on the field of battle... victorious."
Vince Lombardi

_____
_____
_____
_____
_____
_____
_____
_____
_____

"In life it is important to recognize your responsibility to be of service to others and to give back to those who follow in your footsteps."
Lillian Greene-Chamberlain, Ph.D.

_____
_____
_____
_____
_____
_____
_____
_____
_____
_____

"All of us driven by a simple belief that the world as it is just won't do - that we have an obligation to fight for the world as it should be."
First Lady Michelle Obama

_____

_____

_____

_____

_____

Quotes for Inspiration

"The ultimate measure of a man is not where he stands in moments of comfort and convenience, but where he stands at times of challenge and controversy."
Dr. Martin Luther King

_____

_____

_____

_____

_____

_____

"Cautious, careful people, always casting about to preserve their reputations... can never effect a reform."
Susan B. Anthony

_____

_____

_____

_____

"You don't make progress by standing on the sidelines, whimpering and complaining. You make progress by implementing ideas."
Shirley Chisholm

_____
_____
_____
_____
_____
_____
_____
_____
_____

Quotes for Inspiration

"Finish each day and be done with it. You have done what you could. Some blunders and absurdities no doubt crept in; forget them as soon as you can. Tomorrow is a new day; begin it well and serenely and with too high a spirit to be cumbered with your old nonsense."
Ralph Waldo Emerson

_____
_____
_____
_____
_____
_____
_____

"Brethren, I count not myself to have not apprehended; but this one thing I do, forgetting those things which are behind, and reaching forth unto those things which are before."
Philippians 3:13

"Give me six hours to chop a tree and I will take four hours to sharpen the ax."
Abraham Lincoln

Quotes for Inspiration

"There were four people named everybody, somebody, anybody and nobody. There was an important job to be done and everybody was sure that somebody would do it. Somebody got anger about that because it was nobody's job. Everybody thought anybody could do it, but it was nobody who realized that everybody blamed somebody when nobody did what anybody could have done."
Unknown

_____
_____
_____
_____
_____
_____
_____
_____
_____

"Hold fast to your dreams, for without them life is a broken winged bird that cannot fly."
Langston Hughes

_____
_____
_____
_____
_____
_____

Quotes for Inspiration

"You will never make it indeed they thought they were right, but I kept on plodding onwards because I thought I might. You will never make it as the problems multiplied, but I had to make an effort and know at least I tired. So I dug my heels in deeper although my spirits lagged and I shoulder that which was lightest and the rest I kind of dragged. And low to their amazement at the end of the day that which they said I could not I had managed anyway."
Unknown

"Avoid having your ego so close to your position that when your position falls your ego goes with it."
General Colin Powell

"Do not look back and ask why, look forward and ask, why not."
Herbert L. Becker

Quotes for Inspiration

Remember to plant the Garden of Success, in the garden plant 5 rows of "P's":

Purpose, Prepare, Patience, Perturbed, Persevere.

Plant 3 rows of SQUASH, squash criticism, squash gossip, squash indifference.

Plant 6 rows of LETTUCE, let us be respectful, let us be committed, let us be unselfish, let us be truthful, let us be positive and let us be thankful.

Plant 3 rows of ORANGES, aren't you special, aren't you gifted, and aren't you a child of God?

Plant 3 rows of TURN UPS, turn up with an optimistic attitude, turn up with a new idea and turn up with the determination to make this world a better place tomorrow than you did today.

Joetta Clark Diggs

If you maintain this garden you will eventually see the fruits of your labor.

It is my sincere hope that you re-read the quotes and constantly apply them to your life. A space has been created for you to develop your quotes. Have fun, be creative, visit often and remember to express your feelings. I know there is an original quote somewhere within you.

Your Quotes For Inspiration

_____

_____

_____

_____

_____

_____

_____

_____

_____

_____

_____

_____

_____

_____

_____

_____

_____

_____

_____

_____

_____

_____

_____

_____

_____

_____

Your Quotes For Inspiration

_____

_____

_____

_____

_____

_____

_____

_____

_____

_____

_____

_____

_____

_____

_____

_____

_____

_____

_____

_____

_____

_____

_____

_____

_____

_____

Your Quotes For Inspiration

_____

_____

_____

_____

_____

_____

_____

_____

_____

_____

_____

_____

_____

_____

_____

_____

_____

_____

_____

_____

_____

_____

_____

_____

_____

_____

Clark Diggs' Distinctions

1988, 1992, 1996 & 2000 Olympian
Executive Director, Joetta Clark Diggs Sports Foundation
President, Joetta Sports & Beyond
Author, Joetta's *P* Principles for Success
Inducted into the USA Track & Field Hall of Fame
Inducted into the University of Tennessee's Hall of Fame
Garden State Women of the Year, Non Profit 2009
Athletic career spans from 1972-2000
Selected by the Star Ledger as
"NJ Women Athlete of the Century"
2000 USA Olympic Women's Team Captain
Wife and Mother
Daughter of Mrs. Jetta M. Clark
and Dr. Joe Clark, Subject of the Movie
"Lean on Me"
Five Time US Champion in 800m
Ranked top 10 in USA for 21 years
Ranked top 10 in the World over 6 times for 10 years
Member of the National Teams from 1977-2000 USA
15 Time All American, 9 Time NCAA Champion
11 Time All SEC
University of Tennessee, Graduate
Columbia HS Graduate
Currently holds the state record at 800m outdoors 2:03.4
set in 1980
Undefeated in NJ at 800m

www.joettasportsandbeyond.com

Edwards Brothers, Inc.
Thorofare, NJ USA
November 21, 2011